Linda Colley was educated at the Universities of Bristol and Cambridge. She is currently Associate Professor of History at Yale University and a Fellow of the Royal Historical Society. Her *In Defiance of Oligarchy: The Tory Party 1714–1760* appeared to critical acclaim in 1982. She has since published a series of important articles, and is a regular contributor to the *Observer* and to the *London Review of Books*.

Before he died in 1960 Lewis Namier was widely regarded as one of the cleverest and most important historians in the Western world. The word 'Namierism' was enshrined in the English language to describe a distinctive way of writing and thinking about the past. Yet for all his reputation and renown (and perhaps indeed because of them), Namier's diverse writings are today seldom read or properly understood. In this brilliant study Linda Colley re-assesses his contribution to both British and European history. She explores the connections between his troubled and tormented life and the subjects that obsessed him. She examines his intellectual debt to Freudianism, Marxism and Zionism, and argues that Namier must be seen as a social and not just as a political historian. She considers throughout some of the paradoxes that characterized his career. Why did a man who was an outsider in terms of his origins, culture and temperament come to be seen as the pre-eminent historian of England's political elite? Why is his work so often linked with an aversion to ideology, when he himself cherished such fixed ideas? And why have his books and methodologies met with both undue neglect and slavish emulation? How significant and creative a historian was Lewis Namier, in fact?

Historians on Historians

Roy Porter on *Gibbon*
Hugh Tulloch on *Acton*
Owen Dudley Edwards on *Macaulay*
John Gould on *Herodotus*

forthcoming titles
David Cannadine on *Trevelyan*
Nicholas Phillipson on *Hume*
Douglas Johnson on *Michelet*

Namier

By the same author

In Defiance of Oligarchy: The Tory Party 1714–1760

Linda Colley

Lewis Namier

Weidenfeld and Nicolson
London

First published in 1989 by
George Weidenfeld & Nicolson Ltd
91 Clapham High Street, London SW4 7TA

British Library Cataloguing in Publication Data

Colley, Linda, *1949*–
    Namier.
    1. Historiography. Namier, Sir Lewis,
    I. Title
    907'.2024
    ISBN 0-297-79508-2 (cased)
        0-297-79587-2 (paper)

Printed in Great Britain at The Bath Press, Avon

Contents

In memory of
Harriet Fenella Saffron Cannadine
A magical daughter

Acknowledgements

When Sir Lewis Namier was embarking on one of his major works, he called – as historians have frequently to do – for 'Time, Cash and Patience'. In researching and writing this book, I have been lucky enough to enjoy all three commodities. Generous as ever, Yale University supplied the necessary leisure and finance, awarding me a Senior Faculty Fellowship for the 1987–8 academic year. Patience, alas, is not in Yale's gift. But I received it in ample measure from those friends and scholars who responded to my requests for assistance and information. I have to thank the Master and Fellows of Balliol College, Oxford, for allowing me to quote from the published works by Namier of which they hold the copyright. The archivists at the Bodleian Library and at Cambridge and Yale University Libraries provided invaluable aid. Among the many individuals with whom I discussed this project, I owe a particular debt to Constance Babington Smith, Bernard Bailyn, Ian Christie, Peter and Ruth Gay, Peter Hasler, Lucjen Lewitter, R.A.C.Parker, Sir John Plumb, Norman Rose, Quentin Skinner, George and Zara Steiner, Lawrence Stone, D.Cameron Watt and Anne Whiteman. Thanks, too, to Juliet Gardiner and Allegra Huston who handled this book and its author with professionalism, wisdom and wit.

Without David Cannadine, however, neither this book nor the circumstances in which it was written would have been possible.

L.J.C.
March 1988

ix

Chronology

1888   Ludwik Bernsztajn vel Niemirowski born in Russian Poland.

1890   Moves to Austrian Poland.

1906–7   Attends Lausanne University.

1907–8   Comes to England. Attends London School of Economics.

1908–11   Reads history at Balliol College, Oxford.

1913   Becomes British citizen and changes name to Lewis Bernstein Namier. Works in the USA.

1914   Returns to England and joins Royal Fusiliers.

1915   Joins the intelligence service at the Foreign Office. *Germany and Eastern Europe* published.

1917   Marries Clara Sophia Edeleff-Poniatowska. *The Czecho-Slovaks: An Oppressed Minority.*

1921   Clara leaves him. Raises money on the Viennese stock exchange and as a correspondent for the *Manchester Guardian*. Analysed by Theodor Reik.

1922   Father dies. Family estate left to Namier's sister.

1929   *The Structure of Politics at the Accession of George III*. Political Secretary to the Jewish Agency in London.

1930   *England in the Age of the American Revolution.*

1931   *Skyscrapers and Other Essays*. Becomes Professor of Modern History at Manchester University. A.J.P.Taylor is a colleague there later in the decade.

1932   Committee on the Records of Past Members of the House of Commons, of which Namier is a leading member, issues its report.

1934   Delivers Ford Lectures. They are never published in full. Active in rescuing and relocating German-Jewish scholars and students.

1937   *Additions and Corrections to Sir John Fortescue's Edition of the Correspondence of King George III.*

1939   *In the Margin of History.* Adviser to Chaim Weizmann at the Palestine Conference.

1940   Arranges to commit suicide if Nazis invade Britain. Works throughout war on behalf of resistance groups in Europe and for a Jewish state in Palestine.

1942   *Conflicts: Studies in Contemporary History.*
1945   Clara dies.
1946   *1848: The Revolution of the Intellectuals.*
1947   Delivers Waynflete lectures, 'The German problem in 1848–50'. They are never published. Marries Julia de Beausobre. *Facing East.*

1948   *Diplomatic Prelude: 1938–1939.* Lectures on 'Nationality and Liberty' in Rome. Honorary Fellow of Balliol College.

1950   *Europe in Decay: A Study in Disintegration, 1936–1940.*

1951   Member of the Editorial Board of the History of Parliament. Namier's patron, Harold Macmillan, enters the cabinet.

1952   Romanes Lecture: 'Monarchy and the Party System'. Knighted. *In the Nazi Era.*

1953   Retires from Manchester University.
1955   *Personalities and Powers.*
1957   Second edition of *The Structure of Politics at the Accession of George III.*

1958   *Vanished Supremacies: Essays on European History, 1812–1918.*

1960   Dies in London.

1961   Second edition of *England in the Age of the American Revolution.*

1962   *Crossroads of Power: Essays on Eighteenth-Century England.*

1964   *The History of Parliament: The House of Commons 1754–1790* (3 vols.) and *Charles Townshend*: Namier's last works, written in collaboration with John Brooke and others.

1971   Julia Namier's *Lewis Namier: A Biography.*

1976   *Supplement to the Oxford English Dictionary* includes 'Namierian', 'Namierite' and 'Namierization'.

Introduction

Sir Lewis Namier was not just a great historian, he was also recognized in his lifetime and after as one of twentieth-century Britain's foremost academics and intellectuals. When he died in 1960, his memorial service drew peers of the realm. The Prime Minister, Harold Macmillan, sent a personal representative; and Lord Boothby delivered an address loaded with tribute: 'There he stands ... four square, in the line of the greatest British historians. When you think of his origins, and of his life, it makes you pause in awe.'[1] In the following decade a succession of eminent men testified in print to Namier's brilliance and significance. E.H.Carr described him as a 'towering outsider'. Arnold Toynbee remembered him as 'a big man with a big mind'. For A.J.P.Taylor, Namier was 'a historian of genius'; and for Isaiah Berlin, 'one of the most distinguished historians of our time'.[2] If any further confirmation of his status were needed, the compilers of the *Oxford English Dictionary* seemed to provide it. In 1976 they formally acknowledged that the verb 'to namierize', the adjective 'namierian' and the noun 'namierization' had become integral parts of the English language. Probably no other historian, before or since, has been so honoured or had his name so explicitly linked with a way of writing, a way of thinking about history.

Since Namier's impact was so remarkable, we might expect that it would be easy to describe and assess his achievement. Yet this is emphatically not the case. Although books have been written about his life and his involvement in Zionist politics, there has until now been no full-length study of his historical works and method. In part this is because his formidable career is such a recent phenomenon. We may safely agree to admire Clarendon, Gibbon, Hume, Macaulay or Maitland, because the work of such historians has been sanctified and sanitized by the passage of time. Namier, by contrast, is sufficiently modern to be able still to arouse passionate controversy. He was also sufficiently flawed as an individual to make a great many enemies. Even today, there are prominent men and women in the historical profession who had direct experience of his arrogance, or who were savaged in one of his unsigned but unmistakable reviews, or who resented the thought-control and job-control he exercised in the 1950s. The hostility and envy that Namier cultivated in his lifetime have, almost inevitably, worked against his reputation since his death.

Unlike many of his great predecessors, too, Namier has never been widely read or regarded as a grand writer on grand subjects. His prose is often arresting and always distinctive; but he made few concessions to his audience, and none at all to the ignorant or the idle. His most significant work was on eighteenth-century England, a field which had never been fashionable before he applied himself to it and which his writings seemed to make even less accessible. For although he unearthed many new and important truths about this period, he never incorporated them into a general synthesis that ordinary men and women could enjoy and appreciate. Namier found eighteenth-century English history dim with ancient errors; he left it clouded with fresh complexities.

Namier's reputation has also suffered from his failure to complete any of the major projects he embarked upon. The multi-volume epic he planned on England in the age of the American Revolution foundered after the first two volumes. His protracted endeavours to anatomize the eighteenth-century House of Commons were never fully appreciated in his lifetime, and remained unfinished at his death. His suggestive analysis of the Revolutions of 1848 was not expanded, as he once hoped, into a major study. His many essays on nineteenth- and twentieth-century European history remain in essence recycled journalism: 'the nearest substitute I can offer,' as he admitted, 'for the continuous narrative which was originally intended'.[3] Few great historians have been more clever and more obsessively hardworking than Namier; but fewer still have produced so little durable work or so much that was uneven in quality.

It is scarcely surprising, then, that none of his books appeared in paperback in his lifetime (some were even remaindered). Nor is it really surprising that in Britain today all but four of them are out of print. Ever since the 1960s, the most fashionable history among Western scholars has been social history and the history of ideas. Interest in and enthusiasm for accounts of the political manoeuvres of elite groups – the sort of history that Namier is most identified with – has noticeably receded. True, there are signs that in the more conservative 1980s fashions in history are changing once again; but they have yet to change to Namier's benefit. For more than twenty years now, his work has been increasingly dismissed as irrelevant and wrong. It has been read, if read at all, primarily by those seeking to disagree with it. When I was first introduced to eighteenth-century British history in the early 1970s, this was how I learned to approach Namier's books – as ageing and impaired classics whose time had passed.

The pages which follow are not an act of contrition for these earlier views. As will soon become clear, I remain unsympathetic to certain aspects of Namier's historical analysis. But reading him again, I found myself deeply impressed by the sheer exhilarating power of his intelligence, by the range of his insight and by his formidable originality. Now that more than a quarter of a century has elapsed since his death, it should surely be possible not only to recover Namier as a historian but also to discover and interpret him anew. This is the purpose of my book. It does not attempt to vindicate a dead man or to gloss over his evident limitations. Instead it seeks to explore the motives that lay behind his historical work, to establish what was new and important about his methods and discoveries, and to estimate how far his work matters and should matter today.

The next chapter reconstructs what manner of man this was. This is not an easy task since most of Namier's private and historical papers have been lost or destroyed, and many of the extant accounts of him are by men and women who are in some way *parti pris*. Yet unless we understand something of the peculiar circumstances of Namier's life and career, we will not be able to appreciate why his historical writings took the form they did. Chapter 2 examines the intellectual context of Namier's work, and scrutinizes his own ideas and prejudices. These need to be stressed because he has so often been regarded as an opponent of ideology, and as a practitioner of ostentatiously colourless history. In fact, his approach to Britain's past and still more to the history of Western and Eastern Europe was powerfully influenced by his Jewishness, his Freudianism, his reluctant Marxism, his obsession with nationalism, and even his social snobbery. In Isaac Deutscher's captivating phrase, history for Namier was a watch-tower on the world and its issues, not an ivory tower in which to seek refuge from them.

Chapters 3 and 4 concentrate on Namier's most important work, his detailed examination of England's political and social elites in the eighteenth century. They seek to explain why his apparently minute and carefully documented analysis made so great a scholarly impact when it first appeared, and to argue that his approach to English society in this period was far more suggestive and wide-ranging than is now often implied. Finally, I consider past and present verdicts on Namier's quality as a historian, and offer my own assessment of his significance. Of course not everyone will agree with it. Namier was an odd, tormented and elusive man; and in death, as in life, he divides opinion. But this is part of his appeal. He is not securely fixed in the amber of a set and safe academic reputation. Instead, he still causes trouble. He still provokes disagreement. And he still – invariably – makes us think. In Hugh Trevor-Roper's words, his historical writings are 'as fresh as heresy':[4] and heresy is indispensable to life.

1 The Outsider Looking Inwards

> In his moody youth he had imbibed certain
> impressions and arrived at certain conclusions,
> and they never quitted him.
>   (Benjamin Disraeli, *Tancred*)[1]

Historians experience a double existence, simultaneously captivated by the past of which they write and caught up in the present in which they live. It follows that a historian's work – however scholarly and however exact it may be – rarely springs forth pure and unsullied like Pallas Athene. Rather, as Namier himself wrote:

> A great history work becomes, and indeed has to be, part of the life of its author. . . . An intimate knowledge of a past period and the author's own life experience, in matters big and small, must blend, grow and develop (not mingle) together.[2]

In order to come to terms with Namier's history, then, we need to understand something of the man himself, and that is by no means easy.

We can, it is true, learn a great deal from the remarkable biography of him written by his second wife Julia de Beausobre.[3] This won a bevy of literary prizes when it was published in 1971, and is so hauntingly well written and so moving that it compels belief. But it is not an objective account and neither is it a comprehensive one. As Julia admitted, she was not interested in evaluating Namier as a historian. Nor – and this she did not admit – was she qualified to appreciate every aspect of his character. An ardent and proselytizing Christian, she was happier recording Namier's strange and belated conversion to Anglicanism, than she was in analysing the Zionism which had obsessed him since his twenties. Deeply serious, and marked in body and spirit by her experiences in Russian concentration camps in the 1930s, she had no instinctive understanding of the British Establishment which Namier relished, and no great desire perhaps to record his capacity for irony and levity. 'Julia is a mystic,' Namier once confided to some fellow historians, 'I am not.'[4] This was not entirely accurate. But it was the case that Namier had very little interest in spiritual or religious matters in abstract terms. What absorbed him was his own self, and what tortured him throughout his life was his quest for an identity that would hold and endure.

From the beginning, his life was a marginal and deeply ambiguous one. Born in 1888, so frail that he was initially given up as dead, Ludwik Bernsztajn vel Niemirowski spent most of his youth on his family's estates in Eastern Galicia. This was part of Austrian Poland and perilously close to the Russian border. It was an isolated, profoundly rural society in which good roads, railways and industries were virtually unknown, and almost half of the farmland was still controlled by an educated and aloof minority of large landowners:

> Before the war the manor-houses on the big landed estates were centres of high culture and mainstays of modern economic life in Eastern Europe. They resembled Roman villas in semi-barbaric lands. Their inhabitants read the books and thought the thoughts of the most advanced civilization in the midst of an illiterate peasantry.[5]

By the time Namier wrote these lines, in 1922, this way of life had been obliterated for ever. But he was always to retain a strong sense of the power conferred by the possession of land, a paternalistic sympathy with the inarticulate masses of the countryside, and a no less conservative suspicion of towns and of the urban working class.

The bulk of the population in Eastern Galicia was Ukrainian, Catholic and poor; Ludwik's parents by contrast were both prosperous Polonized Jews. His father, Joseph, came from a long line of Talmudic scholars, was himself well educated and had a marked gift for languages that he passed on to his son. He was also temperamentally unstable and a compulsive gambler. Ludwik's mother, Anna, was the daughter of a self-made agricultural entrepreneur, and a much tougher character. Joseph and Anna were alike, however, in their determination to be assimilated into Austrian Poland's social elite. They wanted to distinguish themselves both from the Ukrainian peasantry and from the poorer Yiddish-speaking Polish Jews, the so-called Stetl Jews. Consequently, they refused to allow Ludwik to speak Ukrainian (he disobeyed them of course); they did not practise their Judaism or have him circumcised; they did not even tell him that he was a Jew until he was ten years old. Instead in 1902 they had his eyelids and nose operated on in Vienna, ostensibly to cure his sinuses but perhaps so that he – and they – could more easily be accepted as gentile patricians.[6]

We shall never know how soon and how far Ludwik rebelled against this tense upbringing, or just how tense it really was. Julia's biography describes how father and son were increasingly at odds over politics, religion, education and the family fortune, and gives the impression of two brilliant and difficult personalities locked in a classic Oedipal combat. This was probably how the mature Namier, steeped in Freudian analysis, remembered his childhood. Certainly he seems both to have been obsessed by his father and to have felt belittled by him: hence perhaps his comment that it was an Oxford don (and not either of his parents) 'who first tried to make a man of me'.[7] But we need to be careful. At the time, family relationships may have been less conventionally polarized and rather more complex. 'Strange to read his valuation of his parents,' one of Namier's cousins wrote after Julia's biography was published: 'For us, Anna was *the* outstanding member of the family, full of strength and perseverance. Her drive Lewis inherited. Joseph appeared to us a useless waste, a bore to be tolerated only because of Anna.'[8] Whatever the truth, and there is rarely a monolithic truth in such matters, it is clear that by the time he was eighteen Ludwik had decided to escape from his family and from Eastern Galicia.

It was by no means a foregone conclusion, however, that he would come to Britain and find his life's work there. True, other European options were limited. In 1906 he had gone briefly to Lwow University only to encounter some unpleasant anti-Semitism. Memories of the Dreyfus case in France and of more recent attacks on Jews in Russia and Germany seemed to rule out higher education in those countries also. He could, however, have followed the example of thousands of other Galician Jews at this time and emigrated to the United States. Instead he decided in 1907 to go to London. Seven years earlier, the Fourth Zionist Conference had assembled there, and Theodor Herzl had declared that Britain was one of the few Western nations free of the scourge of anti-Semitism.[9] Ludwik's future career would show that this was not entirely true, but it was sufficiently true to persuade him to become a British subject in 1913 and to change his name to Lewis Bernstein Namier.

The speed with which Namier impressed a variety of powerful men and women in his new country is one of the best testimonies to his striking gifts and persistent ambition. He first enrolled as a student in the London

9

School of Economics, an institution that was still very much under the influence of Beatrice and Sidney Webb and their friends. Namier himself duly became a member of the Fabian Society in November 1907 and this brought him the acquaintance of A.L.Smith, a supporter of the Workers' Educational Association and a prominent history don at Balliol College, Oxford. It was largely thanks to Smith that Namier was admitted to Balliol in 1908, emerging three years later with a first-class degree in modern history. But this was only the beginning. 'All I've done I owe to Balliol,' Namier once remarked: and in a sense this was true. Ever since 1870, when the great Benjamin Jowett became Master, the college had prided itself on placing a disproportionately large number of its alumni in positions of leadership in the British state.[10] It had produced imperial proconsuls such as Curzon, Elgin, Lansdowne and Milner; reared statesmen such as Herbert Asquith, Sir Edward Grey and – later on – Namier's patron, Harold Macmillan; and contributed notable churchmen such as Archbishop Lang, as well as scores of high-ranking figures in the home and overseas Civil Service. His brief sojourn in this hothouse of influence and elitism left a permanent impress on Namier's perception of British society, and ultimately of British history. It produced in him an almost uncritical admiration for the country's ruling class, and strengthened his belief that a highly gifted and homogeneous oligarchy was the political ideal.

Balliol not only showed Namier how others could benefit from an efficient patronage machine, it also helped to supply him with his own patrician supporters. After 1912 his scholarly ambitions were for a time disrupted by the need to make money to pay his father's debts, and subsequently by the Great War. But Oxford and Balliol men were soon able to rescue him. A coterie of influential diplomats, imperialists and gentlemen scholars, including Sir James Headlam-Morley, Lord Eustace

Percy, Sir Cecil Spring-Rice and Sir Reginald Wingate, plucked him out of the British army (where his poor eyesight and guttural accent seemed likely to get him shot by his own side if not by the Germans) and placed him in the intelligence service at the Foreign Office. He was soon attached to the prestigious Political Intelligence Department, earning a comfortable £400 a year, drafting memoranda on Eastern and Central European affairs and assisting in the dissolution of the Austrian Empire at the Paris Peace Conference. In the long term, this direct exposure to political intrigue and diplomatic manoeuvre would enrich Namier's historical work, lending it a degree of authority and confidence denied to most 'don-bred dons'. More immediately, his time at the Foreign Office brought him into fruitful contact with some of the other bright young men it had recruited to fight the war – fellow historians such as E.H.Carr and R.W. Seton-Watson, as well as John Buchan, J.M.Keynes and Harold Nicolson.[11]

Only in the 1920s did Namier's luck – like that of so many men and women in that decade – falter badly. After 1921 he had no academic or state employment. In 1922 his father died, leaving the family estate not to him but to his sister. So Namier had to rely on political journalism and some shrewd speculation in the Viennese money market to support himself and his incessant history-writing. Worst of all he married disastrously. We know that he met Clara Sophia Edeleff-Poniatowska, a Russian refugee, in London in 1916; and his biographer tells us that they drifted into an affair, that she clamoured pathetically for marriage and that he reluctantly agreed. Whether, however, Julia Namier knew or told the whole story about her predecessor is not clear. A.J.P.Taylor, who met Clara, found her fey and enchanting.[12] But she lived in a fantasy world of her own, craved constant attention and almost certainly found her husband's obsessive scholarship a frightening bore. In 1921 she fled. So until her death in 1945 Lewis was left with yet another ambiguity in a life that was already crammed full of them: 'Jew and not Jew, Pole and not Pole, landowner and not landowner,' he was now a married man, but without a wife.[13]

Yet even in this, the bleakest period of his life, Namier never starved in a garret. For most of the time, indeed, he lived in Chelsea and employed a secretary. He was always buoyed up by the contacts he had made in Oxford, and he rarely doubted that at some future time Britain would give him his chance. His choice of a hero at this stage of his life only bears this out. While in Vienna in the early 1920s, he and a close friend Frederick George Steiner clubbed together to buy the six volumes of W.F.Monypenny and G.E.Buckle's *Life of Benjamin Disraeli, Earl of Beaconsfield*. Here was the saga of a Christianized, Anglicized Jew, an oddity and an outsider who had nonetheless defeated prejudice and climbed to the premiership of an empire far larger than that once ruled by the Habsburgs.

Disraeli's career and the ideas he set out in his novels, particularly in *Coningsby* and *Tancred*, were to have a major and prolonged impact on Namier.[14] Like Disraeli, he would come to believe that 'Judaism and Christianity must in the end be reconciled' and to regard himself as a Radical Tory. Like Disraeli, he would devote adulation, nostalgia and the bulk of his writings to the British ruling class. Like Disraeli, too, he would translate the universalism inherent in Judaism into a strong commitment to the worldwide influence of the British Empire.[15] Indeed, his first major publication, *The Structure of Politics at the Accession of George III* (1929), was intended to illuminate the greatest crisis in Britain's early imperial history – the loss of the American colonies. It attracted favourable attention, but it left Namier still without a job. With his second book, however, *England in the Age of the American Revolution* (1930), he was luckier. G.M.Trevelyan, Regius Professor of Modern History at Cambridge University, wrote a review of it for *The Nation*, a review that was both remarkably generous, given Trevelyan's own Whiggish approach to English history, and extremely acute:

> There is a touch of something unique in Mr. Namier, a new method of tasting the intellectual pleasures of history. There are so many different ways in which things happen, or can be truly described as happening. Gibbon's is one, Carlyle's another, Macaulay's a third. Each is true, yet taken by itself each is false, for no one of them is the whole truth. In Mr. Namier's narrative things 'happen' in yet another new way – the Namier way. And it is one of the truths. ... Mr. Namier is a new factor in the historical world.[16]

On the strength of this, Manchester University's history department acted – as British universities were then able and willing to do – with speed, style and imagination. It offered this brilliant unknown quantity its Chair of Modern History and Namier accepted.

Yet he never really appreciated the academic quality and the benevolence of his new employer, nor the personal advantages of working in a city with a large and influential Jewish population. Until his retirement in 1953 he spent the bulk of each week in London. Manchester allowed him to do this, just as it allowed him repeated leaves and sabbaticals to undertake extensive work at the Jewish Agency, and to produce a succession of books, articles and public lectures. These writings were abundant, often incomplete and seemingly erratic, but if we consider them as a whole it is clear that his working life was dominated by two main historiographical obsessions.

The first was what Namier styled the 'Phoenix Empire'. Ever since his time at Balliol and Oxford, he had been fascinated by the dual but connected problems of why Britain had lost the American colonies and why her ruling class and her empire had been able to revive again after 1783. These questions underlay his first two books, the Ford Lectures he delivered at Oxford in 1934 on George III's early cabinets (they were never published in full), his ferocious assault on Sir John Fortescue's sloppy edition of George III's correspondence (1937), his elegant Romanes Lectures on *Monarchy and the Party System* (1952) and, finally, his analysis of the House of Commons between 1754 and 1790, and his psycho-biography of Charles Townshend, both of which were written in collaboration with John Brooke and published after Namier's death.

Namier's second major concern was largely a response to the rise and fall of Nazi Germany. From the early 1930s he increasingly abandoned academic history for active Zionism and political journalism, repeatedly warning against the consequences of German territorial ambitions and rearmament. From these contemporary preoccupations grew a determination to write a history of nineteenth- and twentieth-century Europe that would focus on Germany's national unification and on its violent and global repercussions. Namier outlined the grandeur of this theme most explicitly in his Waynflete Lectures of 1947 which – like the projected history of Europe – were never published or completed: 'The century which has closed is that of German predominance in Europe, the age which has closed is that of European predominance in the world. ... There opens now an extra-European, Europaistic age.'[17]

The sheer ambition of Namier's approach to European history seems far removed from his scrupulously detailed and archivally based British history, yet in fact there were close intellectual links between these two aspects of his work. Namier's understanding of modern Europe was deeply personal and almost Manichean. For him, Britain was the epitome of constitutional wisdom and organic development whereas Germany, Britain's counterpoise, was characterized by violence, chaos and ineptitude. So while his British history was very much a celebration of the country's governing elite and political pragmatism, his European history was in essence an inquiry into why Eastern and Western European states had so conspicuously failed to replicate Britain's comparative social and political stability, freedom from militarism and territorial integrity. Why had those European dynasties and aristocracies which had collapsed in the face of German ambition not been able to adapt and endure as Britain's rulers had done? Namier addressed these issues in a plethora of incisive, polemical but still pertinent newspaper articles (many of which were reprinted as collected essays), and in a series of lectures: '1848: The Revolution of the Intellectuals' (the Raleigh Lecture of 1944), his Waynflete Lectures on 'The German Problem 1848–50' delivered in 1947, a lecture in Rome the following year on 'Nationality and Liberty', and his Creighton Lectures of 1952 on 'Basic Factors in Nineteenth-Century European History'.

This string of prestigious public lectures demonstrates just how fortunate and successful Namier's historical career in the end became. Time and time again his genius was widely recognized by other scholars and richly rewarded. And in the last decade of his life, he received the more secular and honorific bouquets with which Britain traditionally acknowledges the acceptable face of achievement. There was a knighthood in 1952, and a succession of honorary degrees from the Universities of Oxford, Cambridge and Durham. Had he been a different kind of man, or had he been interested only in history, he could surely have gone into the good night if not gently then at least with a certain warm complacency. Yet he did no such thing. Although an intensely happy second marriage and the worldly successes of his old age made him more mellow, he remained all his life a passionate, controversial and essentially joyless man. He had no children. He had no taste for the theatre or music or any consuming cultural interest that might have distracted him from his incessant work. He suffered increasingly from deafness and insomnia, and was haunted by the fear of insanity.[18] And he was always prone to self-pity, inclined both to see himself as the victim of various forms of persecution and to indulge in bouts of introspective self-hatred: 'I am the doyen of the rejected,' he declared just seven years before his death and, on another occasion, 'What a mess I've made of my life.'[19]

The reasons for this annihilating bitterness lay in his circumstances as well as his temperament. Because he ardently desired the approval of what is commonly called the British Establishment, that labyrinthine and essentially masculine edifice of clubs and interlinking societies, he was extremely vulnerable to any ostracism by it. In some ways Oxbridge did ostracize him. All Souls turned him down for a fellowship in 1911. Balliol made no effort to retain his services after 1921. Before and after the Second World War, he was repeatedly passed over for Chairs at both ancient universities. It is probable that anti-Semitism and anti-Zionism played a part in all this.[20] Anyone who doubts that should glance at his obituary in the London *Times* in 1960. Namier, remarked the safely anonymous writer, could be a ferocious polemicist, and 'the crushing blow was the more unexpected from being delivered with a special Jewish dexterity'.[21]

Yet, as even this comment suggests, discrimination was only part of Namier's problem. Although lovable and brilliant to those few people who knew him well, and kind and attentive to a growing number of research students and disciples, he was undoubtedly rude, contemptuous and arrogant to critics and to those (a great many) whom he regarded as second-rate. He could also very easily seem a monumental bore. Physically big, with hooded, penetrating eyes, he spoke with a heavy East European accent and he spoke a great deal. Arnold Toynbee once recalled being cornered on some icy college stairs while Namier recounted at length the original Slavonic names of various German towns.[22] Toynbee of course was fascinated, but there were many who were not. Dealing with Namier, wrote the Master of Pembroke, left one with a 'sense of pulverized resentment'; while another Oxford man confided to Rebecca West that 'he and his kind had for years prevented Sir Lewis Namier from getting a Chair', in part because he 'talked too much'.[23] An immensely clever Jew he might be; but perhaps too clever, and just think how he would behave at dinner.

But even if Oxbridge had been more accommodating, it is doubtful if Namier would ever have felt at peace with himself. There were simply too many divergent strands in his life. Part of him yearned for Poland, and for the family lands in Galicia which were finally lost to the Communists after 1945. And part of him badly needed to make sense of his Jewishness, which was both immensely precious to him and also a crushing burden. He never learned Hebrew; he rarely attended a synagogue; and, at his lowest, he tended to believe that the Jewish problem was insoluble: 'They just must stop breeding and the race will die out painlessly. It would be best.'[24] But his awareness of his Jewish heritage and of the degree to which it had moulded his own nature never let him go. The Jew, he wrote once, is 'continually on trial and under examination':

Harried, he is blamed for being restless; kept out or kept down, he is described as pushing and assertive; hurt, he searches for compensations and is called vain, blatant, or self-indulgent; insecure, he yearns for standing, power, and wealth: which sometimes protect him, but more often expose him the more to attack.[25]

Namier had met the great Chaim Weizmann as early as his student days at Balliol, and the close relationship that developed between them after 1919 only confirmed his belief that assimilation was no solution to this agony. His parents had been wrong in thinking that their ethnic origins could or should be smothered: Jews must have the option of their own territory, their own national identity. In 1929 he joined the Zionist Organization as Political Secretary to its Jewish Agency in London, a job that consumed a large part of his time, energy and emotions until the end of the Second World War.[26]

Few of Namier's co-workers ever had cause to doubt his ability or commitment, but predictably many found him infuriating. He was as naive, difficult and arrogant in political negotiation as he was in academic intrigue. Moreover, his vision of a Jewish state was a highly individual and idiosyncratic one. Always convinced that the American colonists had made a bad mistake in embracing independence back in 1776, Namier hoped that Israel at least could be kept within the British Empire. Its real and violently anti-British genesis appalled him, not least because it seemed to symbolize the incompatibility of his own Britishness and Jewishness. This was one reason why he joined the Anglican Church in 1947, a decision which shocked his Zionist friends (Weizmann is reputed to have cut him dead at the Athenaeum) but which needs to be seen in part as the rather pathetic gesture of a deprived and disappointed man.[27]

Zionist activity had one very obvious impact on Namier's historical writing: it limited the time he could actually give to it. Women were another persistent and self-imposed drain on his energies. Was it unconscious self-revelation or was it tongue-in-cheek humour which made him characterize England's borough constituencies in the eighteenth century as faithful wives, kept mistresses and common prostitutes?[28] Whatever the explanation, Namier knew what he was talking about. He was always sexually driven and in his time experienced all three forms of consolation. Women not only compensated for his worldly failures, they were also patient enough or passive enough to listen to him and support him. Some of his earliest friends in Britain were feminists like Tegan Harris, Rachel Barrett and Rebecca West; his closest ally in the 1920s and 1930s was Blanche Dugdale, Balfour's niece, who arranged financial support when he had no university job and who introduced him to his publishers, Macmillans; and it was to a woman – his second wife – that he explicitly and very wisely entrusted the task of writing his biography. It is pleasant to record that Namier always recognized his debt to women and to some degree repaid it. Of all his protégés in eighteenth-century British history, the one for whom he had the greatest respect was Lucy Sutherland.[29] In 1957 he broke every precedent by recommending her for the Regius Chair of History at Oxford University. Seventeen years later, Balliol awarded its first Sir Lewis Namier Junior Research Fellowship to a female historian. Lewis, wrote Julia, would have been delighted: and so he probably would.[30]

This, then, was Namier's life, a peculiar, diverse and richly cosmopolitan one in comparison with most other distinguished British historians. But how far do all or any of these personal details matter when we assess Namier's work and quality as a historian? In my own opinion, a great deal. There is no doubt, for instance, that his difficult and unconventional career and temperament help to explain why his books appeared so erratically, and why so many of them were never completed at all. Moreover, Namier's persistent sense of himself as an outsider, as a man who had to struggle, influenced his choice of subjects. On the one hand, he was drawn to the political and social elites of the past, towards men who had governed and lived with all 'the uncontending ease, the unbought grace of life'[31] that he himself so conspicuously lacked. On the other, his awareness of the acute difficulties of life gave him insight – some might say too much insight – into the personalities and perplexities behind the power. The brilliant word-pictures he was to create of men as diverse as Metternich, Napoleon, George III and the Duke of Newcastle, were founded in large part on his own capacity to look unhappily but relentlessly at what lay within himself.

More generally it can be argued that Namier's insecurity and anxiety make him one of the most representative and illuminating of all of twentieth-century Europe's great historians. Not only did he labour under a heavy burden of personal angst, but his life also spanned the end of European supremacy and the dissolution of two great empires – first the Habsburg and then the British. If the bulk of Namier's writings is a relentless inquiry into how men can consort together – a scrutiny of the bonds of race and class and nation, and of collective institutions like the House of Commons – this is surely understandable. These matters preoccupied him because the Old World was falling apart as he wrote, and because like so many other creative men and women in Europe this century he himself was never able properly to consort with anyone.

2   The Mind of
the Historian

> How limited is human reason. ... Man is only
> truly great when he acts from the passions;
> never irresistible but when he appeals to the
> imagination.
> (Benjamin Disraeli, *Coningsby*)[1]

Exploring the ideas that lay behind Namier's historical
work may seem a perverse, even a pointless exercise.
He is after all most commonly remembered for his scepti-
cism about the impact of abstract theory on events, and
for his insistence instead on the vital importance of
material interests. His works are littered with expressions
of sovereign contempt for the ideological pretensions of
politicians. Edmund Burke dealt in 'cant'; his opponent
George III in 'flapdoodle'. Radical intellectuals who
relied on systems, he wrote on one occasion, 'often produce mere junk'. As for the generality of mankind, 'It
is a mistake to suppose that [they] think: they wobble
with the brain.'[2] Not all of these statements were
intended to be taken seriously, but they have inevitably
fostered accusations that Namier emptied the history of
politics of all principle. As A.J.P.Taylor, pithy as ever,
expressed it: Namier took the mind out of history.[3]

Some more conservative commentators have viewed
Namier's reputed antipathy towards ideas as a source
of virtue and not as a fault. He has been seen – as he
sometimes saw himself – as a historian in the nineteenth-
century German tradition: objective, concentrating only
on facts, immersed in documentary sources and solely
preoccupied with past politics; in short, as Britain's

answer to Leopold von Ranke.[4] J.P.Kenyon, for example, has presented Namier as the touchstone of professional history, as the prime exponent of a purely scientific approach towards the subject. G.R.Elton, too, has commended Namier for 'studying history – trying to find out – not promoting a personal point of view, or merely (as some do) wishing to create a stir by being different'.[5] But is this correct? Was his history really so pure and so impersonal in fact?

There can be no doubt that Namier was a thorough professional in his art and a consummate scholar. He was one of the first historians of Britain ever to hunt out family manuscripts in a sustained and systematic fashion – his 'paper-chases' as he called them. He was obsessed with accurately dating and comparing relevant documents. And he despised any kind of amateurism. The relish with which he exposed the sloppiness of others is evident throughout his work, but it can be seen most easily in some of his shorter essays. When poor C.W. Everett produced a new edition of the letters of Junius in 1927, and claimed that this anonymous eighteenth-century political journalist was in fact the Earl of Shelburne, Namier pounced and demolished the theory in just three pages. He analysed the content and the timing of the letters themselves, and then used newspapers and family documents to track down Shelburne's actual whereabouts when they were being written. His conclusion was clear, pitiless and apt: 'In short, the author of the Junius "Letters" was in or near London in June, July, and August 1771, when Lord Shelburne was travelling in France and Italy. The bottom falls out of Mr Everett's theory.'[6]

Yet rigorous scholarship even of this daunting quality is not in itself a guarantee of objectivity. Namier, at least, had sufficient insight and integrity to acknowledge this:

Really intense research and analysis requires some correlation between the student's emotional life and experience and his subject. ... As for accuracy, it is a conception that I would associate with statements rather than with views.[7]

In other words, he recognized that however assiduous and however careful historians might be (and it was their duty to be both), their work would inevitably contain an element of autobiography. What they chose to write about, and how they approached their topic, would always be influenced by their experience, by their temperament and — most of all — by the ideas with which they had come in contact. That is why it is legitimate and indeed indispensable to examine what Namier believed and why.

His mind was forged in the quarter-century before the First World War. If we were rash enough to characterize this era by one word, it would have to be 'Anxiety': anxiety caused by sporadic economic depression and by ever-increasing industrial, colonial and strategic competition among nations; anxiety fostered by social change, as old elites began to disintegrate and the masses came increasingly to be enfranchised, educated and crowded together in great cities; and anxiety nurtured by the advent of new technologies and new ideas. Intelligent men and women both in Europe and in the United States began to speculate how, in these shifting conditions, social cohesion could be maintained. They no longer believed — as many of their Victorian forbears genuinely had done — in the steady, orderly progress of prosperity, knowledge and liberal constitutionalism. Instead they felt that their world was changing uncontrollably and that they needed new political and intellectual strategies in order to deal with it.[8]

One very common response was to seek refuge in hard facts, which seemed to offer a measure of certainty amid the flux. In the realm of psychology, Sigmund Freud collected patients who would supply empirical evidence of the more irrational tendencies of mankind and so make possible their correction. Philanthropists and social investigators such as William Booth, Seebohm Rowntree and Sidney and Beatrice Webb accumulated reams of quantitative data on the state of the poor and on the structure of local government. In architecture, the modernists sought to purge buildings of the flamboyance and superficial decoration associated with Art Nouveau, and to create instead only clean, unadorned, factual form. In the fields of science and philosophy, the Austrian Ernst Mach was equally insistent on 'economy of thought', on the need to divorce the laws of physics from metaphysical speculation. And in historical writing, the emphasis – as Richard Hofstadter has argued – was on *reality*: 'Reality was the inside story. It was rough and sordid, hidden and neglected, and being hard and material and inexorable, was somehow more important than mere ideas and theories.'[9]

It was in this spirit of remorseless realism that the great American historian Charles Beard interpreted his country's constitution not as the product of elevated ideology or of an epic struggle for liberty, but rather as a pragmatic document devised and imposed by powerful economic interest-groups in the new republic. It was in this same spirit that A.D.Lindsay at Oxford and E.R.A. Seligman in the United States stressed how important it was for historians to collect economic data and to understand economic forces. These men were not Marxists – indeed they explicitly distanced themselves from Marx's politics and philosophical system – but they were attracted by aspects of his historical materialism. Among contemporary sociologists, the Frenchman Emile Durkheim, the German Max Weber and the Italian Vilfredo Pareto, there was a similar desire 'to give non-Marxian answers to Marxian questions'.[10] In particular they, and many others like them, wanted to explore the connection between social class and political status. This is perfectly understandable if we remember the social changes and disruptions that were occurring at this time. Pareto and Weber were interested in studying elite groups precisely because in the late nineteenth and early twentieth centuries the traditional landed elites of Europe – of which Namier himself was a very minor product – were visibly beginning to disintegrate and to lose confidence and authority.

Namier, in fact, was a classic product of this pre-First World War milieu. We can see this very clearly if we examine his early intellectual development. His first political arguments were with his father, whose favourite philosopher was the Victorian liberal John Stuart Mill. Like many other precocious young men all over Europe at this time, Namier would reject liberalism, just as he would reject his father. He was introduced to Marxism by his private tutors in Eastern Galicia; and though he swiftly discarded socialist doctrine, he retained all his life a tendency towards economic determinism and an interest in the correlation between political decision-makers and their social and economic background. In 1906–7 he spent several months at Lausanne University, and while there attended a course of sociology lectures given by Pareto. These probably only confirmed his pre-existing belief in the inevitability and desirability of some kind of oligarchy. Certainly one of his earliest publications in England was an essay entitled 'A l'Amour du Vieux Monde' (1912), a nervous lament – entirely typical of its period – on the volatility and irrationality of London's masses, and on the threat that they posed to patrician cultural values.[11] Namier spent the year before the war in the United States, and we know that while he was there he read and was much impressed by Charles Beard's *The Economic Origins of the American Constitution* (1912) and *The Economic Origins of Jeffersonian*

Republicanism (1913).[12] His enthusiasm for exploring the economic bases of political events had already been nurtured at Balliol, where his tutors had included the Fabian don A.D.Lindsay.

As we have seen, some of Namier's earliest contacts in England were with members of the Fabian Society. It was probably the political psychologist Graham Wallas who influenced him most, particularly by way of his little classic *Human Nature in Politics*, which appeared in 1908, a year after Namier had arrived at the London School of Economics where Wallas lectured.[13] In this book Wallas stressed the importance of looking below the surface of political convictions: 'Most of the political opinions of most men are the result not of reasoning tested by experience, but of unconscious or half-conscious inference fixed by habit.' Political behaviour could not be understood by reference to intellectual systems, but only by seeking out 'as many relevant and measurable facts about human nature as possible'.[14] Namier had little time for Wallas's socialism, but he did make his book into something of a bible. After a second edition was published in 1948, he wrote a long review applauding its rejection of the independent power of ideas. Ideas only mattered to the extent that men and women held them, and as such they were bound to be subordinated to human instincts and emotions:

> To treat them [ideas] as the offspring of pure reason would be to assign to them a parentage about as mythological as Pallas Athene. What matters most is the underlying emotions, the music, to which ideas are a mere libretto, often of very inferior quality.[15]

This was to be Namier's position in all of his historical writing, whether it was about Georgian England, nineteenth-century Europe, Soviet Russia or Nazi Germany. He never denied that ideas existed: he was in fact appalled at their power to disturb individuals and disrupt societies. But he did not believe that historians should take expressed ideas at their face value. The key to individual and group behaviour had always to be sought in human nature. And how was one to come to grips with this amorphous quantity? Again, Namier found the answer in his own intellectual background. He looked to Wallas, who had stressed the importance of psychology, and he looked to Vienna. He looked above all to Sigmund Freud.

In the early 1920s Namier was analysed in Vienna by Theodor Reik, one of Freud's pupils, and thereafter became something of a psychoanalyst's groupie, moving from couch to couch in search of experience rather than a cure.[16] Residence in Britain proved no barrier to this exploration. In 1910 when he was up at Oxford the British Psychological Society met there to discuss, among other things, 'The Psychology of Freud and His School'. In the 1920s and 1930s the Hogarth Press, under the direction of Leonard and Virginia Woolf, issued English translations of many of Freud's works. Namier benefited from the interest that these aroused, but since he was fluent in German he made his own translations. Some of these still survive among his papers.[17] There is a telling extract from Freud's 'Gradiva' (1907) on 'the ease with which our intellect is prepared to accept something absurd provided it satisfies emotional impulses', and a sentence from 'Family Romances' (1909): 'the whole progress of society rests upon the opposition between successive generations'. These aspects of Freud's thought – his insistence on the interconnection between unconscious emotion and conscious thought, and on the inevitability of conflict between generations, particularly between father and son – profoundly influenced Namier's historical analysis.

Equally important was the attention that psychoanalysis focused on the individual. Namier reconciled his positivism and his Freudianism[18] by insisting throughout his work that historical institutions and movements should ideally be studied *at the level of the individual*, and that historians must find out as many hard facts as possible about each and every person who was involved. This insistence showed itself in Namier's choice of subjects: classically, in his attempt to establish why each man elected to the British House of Commons between 1754 and 1790 wanted to get into Parliament. But it also shaped his historical methods. Throughout his career he avidly tracked down and dissected the diaries, the memoirs and the letters of the individuals who obsessed him. His most important book on twentieth-century Europe, for example – *Diplomatic Prelude* (1948) – is almost entirely based on the testimonies of the accused at the Nuremberg Trials, and on memoirs and apologias published by European statesmen. This was the kind of evidence that fascinated Namier. He was rarely interested in administrative or legal papers, in controversial pamphlets, in sermons or in newspapers. But when he found his individual sources, he cherished them:

> If a man writes a dozen letters to different correspondents on the same day, even on quite different subjects, the subjects and letters will interact, and turns and expressions, attitudes and moods, will lead across from one to the other producing otherwise inexplicable patterns. It is in the psyche of the writer that these things are focussed and from which they radiate.[19]

Hence in part Namier's insistence on the careful editing of historical correspondence, and his practice of incorporating extensive quotations from his sources in his text. Acting in this way was not just careful scholarship, it was indispensable if the historian was properly to convey the characters that he or she was dealing with.

It was of course difficult adequately to psychoanalyse the dead, however well documented they were; but Namier did his best. In England he regularly called on the services of one Dr M.J.Mannheim, a graphologist who was acquainted with Freud's work and who was willing to analyse the handwriting of the past as well as of the present. Namier took his reports very seriously and frequently incorporated their drift in his own historical writing. Thus on one occasion he sent him some letters by Edmund Burke, and was informed that the Irishman's outstanding trait was aggression: 'His closeness to a minority group is in fact an attack on the majority and not closeness to the minority.' As for the penmanship of the man who devised the Stamp Act, George Grenville, 'Spacing of words not good,' Mannheim assured Namier: 'This seems to indicate lack of detachment, perspective, foresight' – an assessment which even a non-graphologist might endorse.[20]

It is easy to mock, and some of Namier's methods positively invite mockery. But his belief that the political and social life of societies can best be approached through a study of the individuals involved deserves to be taken seriously. This was an approach that he judged particularly appropriate in the case of Britain in the second half of the eighteenth century. For here was a country with no written constitution and, for much of this time, no stable political parties. Consequently, Namier believed, only an exploration of its leading personalities would enable one to understand and assess its politics. And the cast of personalities was a particularly rich and well-documented one. There was George III, popularly regarded as sporadically insane; there was the Duke of Newcastle, whom many contemporaries had dismissed as both pathetic and eccentric but who clung to high political office for some forty years; and then there was the brilliant but unstable Charles Townshend, whose financial legislation proved such an irritant in Anglo-American relations in the 1760s.

Namier set about studying these men with a will and with considerable sensitivity. In place of George III the scheming and unbalanced tyrant, his books and essays presented a forlorn individual whose upbringing had allowed him to come to the throne burdened with ill-informed idealism and with a persistent sense of guilt.[21] More generally, he pointed out that a large element of court politics in Britain between 1714 and 1820 derived from the struggles between successive Hanoverian kings and their heirs apparent: George I quarrelled with the future George II; George II bickered with his son Frederick, Prince of Wales, and then again with his grandson, who became George III; the latter monarch was to get on just as badly with his eldest son, the future George IV. Earlier historians had of course noticed these individual and family tensions, but had tended to be either amused by or censorious of them. By contrast, Namier's Freudianism encouraged him to consider their political impact seriously and at length.[22]

It also made it easier for him to assess the Duke of Newcastle, which was by no means a simple or a paltry achievement. Here was a great landed magnate, who had exercised political power since 1717 and who was still enjoying the highest office in 1762, who had a large band of supporters in the House of Commons and who was gifted enough to organize the necessary finance for Britain's military and naval conquests in the Seven Years' War. Yet, as his copious letters demonstrated, he always felt embattled, inadequate and bullied. In the maturity of his career, the task of writing a one-page letter to the Town Clerk of Bristol – a nobody – still took him three drafts and several consultations with the Lord Chancellor. How could such a man hang on to power for such a long time? Why did he even want to do so?

The answer to these questions, Namier believed, could not be found in the realm of reason as it was conventionally understood, but only in psychoanalysis:

> Men are said to seek pleasure and shun pain; but as 'there is no accounting for tastes', the statement is tautological – they seek what they seek. ... There are men who crave for mortification. ... But unless this desire assumes a standardised religious form – hairshirt or hermit's hut – and can be represented as a profitable bargain for another world, men dare not admit it, not even to themselves. ... There was unconscious self-mortification in Newcastle's tenure of office.[23]

How we react to statements like this will probably depend on how far we accept that Freudianism can be a valuable historical tool. Almost all of Namier's disciples – however devoted they might be in general – have rejected this part of the master's method out of hand.[24] Yet Namier's grasp of psychology did enable him to portray eighteenth-century Britons in a peculiarly vivid and compelling fashion. His delight in dissecting and explaining personalities gives readers a rich and immediate sense of what it was like to live and work at a certain intricate level of politics. And insofar as Namier's ideas and methods *detracted* from his historical achievement, it is largely because he never worked out all the historiographical implications of Freudian analysis, or how to combine it with the other skills that good political history requires.

Thus in linking political ideas so absolutely to human nature, Namier never really explained why – since presumably human nature is a constant – the form and content of political ideas change over time. Indeed his penchant for individual analysis often made him write rather static history. Almost all his books and essays are broken up by long biographical excursions. These are brilliantly done, but they tend to prevent him from reaching the proper end of his story. Narrative, the most basic of all the historian's skills, was often beyond Namier's reach. 'I suffer from a very imperfect sense of time,' he admitted in the preface to *The Structure of Politics at the Accession of George III*, and he was right. Planned as the first volume of a magisterial survey on 'The Imperial Problem During the American Revolution', this book and its only sequel stop in 1763 – some twelve years before the Revolution's outbreak.

It can also be argued that Namier's fascination with psychoanalysis, together with his own troubled temperament, led him to concentrate too much on historical figures who were manifestly flawed, inadequate or second-rate. No one has ever captured the essence of the Duke of Newcastle or even of George III better than Namier did: probably no one ever will. But he never applied the same degree of sensitivity and insight, the same grasp of the unconscious, to indubitably great men like George Washington or Pitt the Elder. True, he did on one occasion tackle Napoleon. He showed very cleverly that the single give-away phrase, 'My health is good, my affairs are going well,' appeared with increasing regularity in Napoleon's letters to his wife after 1812, an 'unconscious dirge' that marked the stages of his subsequent decline.[25] But could he have analysed the Emperor's rise and apotheosis with the same degree of perception? Certainly he never tried, any more than he ever tried to come to grips with a genuine ideologue such as Edmund Burke, or with a dazzling extrovert like Charles James Fox. Namier liked his subjects to be in the shadows.

The limitations of Namier's biographical analysis were compounded by his lack of interest in sources that would illuminate administration and policy rather than the individuals behind them. His word-pictures of politicians always reveal a great deal about their character and intrigues, but often fail to show how they used their power to govern. This emerges most clearly in his biography of Charles Townshend, a jointly written, posthumously published and profoundly unsatisfactory book. Namier saw Townshend with great penetration:

> Rigid in his ideas and devoid of intuitive awareness, he was apt to misjudge situations. He did not change or mellow; nor did he learn by experience; there was something ageless about him; never young, he remained immature to the end. He went through life in the mould into which his young years had cast him.[26]

He conveyed in great detail Townshend's unhappy upbringing, his tortured relationship with his father and his deeply ambiguous attitudes to his mother. As a result, he certainly allows his readers to understand far more clearly than before why such a brilliantly gifted and ambitious man had such an erratic and controversial career. But he never explains the legislative or financial background of the Townshend Acts, nor their impact on the colonies. Indeed we are left with the impression that perhaps the American Revolution broke out because Britain in the 1760s was governed by an oligarchy of neurotics. There may of course be some truth in this, but surely not the whole truth?

We have seen how the form and content of Namier's writings on British history were partly determined by his intellectual preconceptions. His ideas and his bias are even more evident in his work on Continental Europe. Not that this work lacks scholarly underpinning. Many of the research notes that Namier assembled in preparation for his Waynflete Lectures on 'The German Problem 1848–1850' have survived and can be seen today at the Bodleian Library in Oxford.[27] They demonstrate just how hard and rigorously he worked. There are drafts which reveal how relentlessly he polished his prose and refined his argument; transcripts and old library application forms which show that he consulted relevant books and articles in all of the major European languages; and page after page of the biographical information that he compiled on the 831 men who were elected to the Frankfurt Parliament in 1848. Namier was a fine and painstaking historical technician. But he was also a polemicist. This emerges with absolute clarity in his treatment of nationalism and Germany, for Namier the two dynamic forces in modern European history.

He approached nineteenth-century European nationalism in characteristic fashion. Not for him a detailed analysis of the political thought of Rousseau, the Abbé Sieyès, Herder or Mazzini. Nor was he interested in the cultural history of nationalism: its connection with developments in language, literature, art and music. Instead he concentrated on those whom he saw as the victims and villains of nationalist movements – the rootless, ill-educated urban masses who manned the barricades or died on the battlefield – and the intellectuals, generals and politicians who exploited their ignorance and enthusiasm. In his youth, Namier had been profoundly sympathetic towards embattled peoples like the Ukrainians and the Czechs who were striving to assert their ethnic and linguistic independence in the face of Austrian, Polish and Russian ambitions.[28] But his mature writings, particularly his *1848: The Revolution of the Intellectuals*, and his superb essay on 'Nationality and Liberty', invariably present nationalism as the prime engine of Europe's subversion and ultimately of its decline.

Namier distinguished between territorial nationalism, a conservative force in which a people identified with a stretch of land long held by their ancestors (England was the prime example here, but perhaps he was also thinking of Palestine) and linguistic nationalism in which men and women aspired to union with those who shared their language or their culture, irrespective of what territory they might live in. The linguistic and cultural confusion of nineteenth-century Europe made it almost inevitable that this second variety of nationalism would lead to armed conflict, the mobilization of the masses, ruthless change and indiscriminate destruction:

> National feeling was hailed in 1848 as a great and noble force which was to have regenerated Europe ... but from the outset it was the expression of social and political maladjustments, and has since been at least as much the vehicle as the source of destructive passions.[29]

A movement that had once been linked with individual liberty in fact destroyed the stability and the peace on which – Namier believed – real liberty depended.

The conservatism here is evident. Namier was in part lamenting the destruction of the older, more cosmopolitan European aristocracies which had been obliterated by nationalism, and by men like Napoleon and Bismarck, who had channelled national enthusiasms into military conquest. But, despite his bias, Namier's sweeping, almost apocalyptic vision has considerable force. For whether the old world that was destroyed was worth preserving or no, it is arguable that what replaced it was a set of powerful and aggressive nation-states which utilized the new technology to mount a series of ever more destructive wars. The culmination of these conflicts – the First and Second World Wars – together undermined Europe, the good along with the bad. Namier himself had no doubt that the good had suffered more:

> Looking back, converted though we cannot be to the *ancien régime*, to the 'system Metternich' or to

Tsarism, we no longer exult over the age of nationality and democracy and its victories. All past social superiorities have been wiped out behind the Iron Curtain, and most of the cultural values which the educated classes had created.[30]

Both Namier's consuming interest in nationalism and his belief that it had acted as a moral infection in the European body politic can be seen in his treatment of the revolutions of 1848. These catered to all of Namier's prejudices. They were explicitly nationalist in inspiration and rhetoric, and so invited his condemnation. They were essentially urban phenomena, and he distrusted towns. They were led by ideologues, intellectuals and academics who enjoyed dabbling in politics: and Namier – an ideologue, an intellectual and an academic who enjoyed dabbling in politics – had no patience with such creatures. Most of all, the revolutions of 1848 attracted Namier because, in contrast with the American, French and Russian revolutions, they had manifestly failed.

Yet although Namier's approach to 1848 was strongly influenced by his own conservatism, his analysis of these revolutions was similar in many respects to that put forward by Karl Marx and Friedrich Engels. He disliked the nationalism of 1848 because he regarded it as destructive; they disliked it because they believed that it was a distraction from class consciousness. He was unconcerned about the ideas of plebeian insurgents and therefore stressed, as Marx and Engels did, the economic forces behind mass action:

Even in southwestern Germany, on the confines of France and Switzerland, feudal survivals were fomenting agrarian revolt. All over Europe independent artisans were fighting their drawn-out losing battle against modern industry. ... On the other hand, the new class of factory workmen was starting its fight for a human existence. . . . Here was plenty of inflammable matter in ramshackle buildings.[31]

Like Marx and Engels, too, Namier was contemptuous of those petty bourgeois dissidents in France and Germany who had sought to cash in on mob revolt in 1848, while also striving nervously to contain it: 'They wanted the revolution to enter like the ghost in Dickens' *Christmas Carol*,' was his pungent judgement, 'with a flaming halo round its head and a big extinguisher under its arm.'[32]

The most ludicrous manifestation of this muted, middle-class protest, Namier claimed, was the Frankfurt Parliament which assembled in May 1848. The bulk of its 831 members had been academicians: no fewer than thirteen of the thirty members of its constitutional committee, Namier calculated, had been university professors.[33] Men of this stamp were naive, timid and ineffectual; they believed that they could influence the rulers of the German states and effect a united Germany by means of talk and written constitutions: 'States are not created or destroyed, and frontiers redrawn or obliterated, by argument and majority votes; nations are freed, united, or broken by blood and iron.'[34] Moreover, Namier contended, these otherwise placid parliamentarians had shown themselves more eager to expand Germany's territorial boundaries than to respect the rights and independence of other nationalities: 'most of the extravagant German claims of the two World Wars were raised and applauded by the "freedom-loving" *idéologues* of the Frankfurt Parliament of 1848'; Hitler could have found 'a great deal to extol' in their work.[35] The unfairness of much of this analysis should be patent. On the one hand, Namier echoed Bismarck and condemned the Frankfurt Assembly for having confined itself to the realm of ideas. On the other, he castigated it for having anticipated twentieth-century German armed aggression. He also chose to ignore completely some of the Parliament's more enlightened initiatives – for example its members' almost unanimous rejection of legal discrimination against the Jews.[36]

Namier's treatment of the 1848 revolutions, then, was widely informed but at best partial. One of the main reasons for this was his hatred of Germany, which was confirmed by the Holocaust but anticipated it by many years. As early as 1915 he had written that 'even the cruelty of a tartar does not approach that of a German', and compared Germany to an octopus incessantly stretching its tentacles into Europe in order to feed itself.[37] He looked back to eighteenth- and nineteenth-century European history, and naturally enough found his prejudices confirmed. From Catherine the Great onwards, he argued, German immigrants into Russia had taken the lead in making it more centralized, more dangerous and more prone to Jewish pogroms. Moreover, Germany had served as the stud farm of Europe. Careful marriages into almost all of the ruling dynasties of Europe had enabled German princes and princesses to tamper with its diplomacy and domestic policies for generations.[38] There had, he admitted, been some German liberals in the nineteenth century, but they had been few in number, often Jewish, or – as in 1848 – notoriously inept. The bulk of Germans were quite simply incapable of freedom.

It was thus no accident that whereas French and Dutch Calvinism, English Puritanism and Scottish Presbyterianism had all served as 'nurseries of self-government and democracy', Lutheranism, 'the German national form of Protestantism ... enjoins obedience to the territorial ruler'.[39] The character of the German people was towards subservience at home and aggression abroad. Consequently the Third Reich had not been 'a gruesome accident or a monstrous aberration, but the correct consummation of the German era in history'; Hitler was not a uniquely evil man who had led a nation astray, but 'probably one of the most representative Germans that ever lived'.[40] In fact, of course, Hitler was an Austrian. But this was a distinction without a difference as far as Namier was concerned. For him, Germans and Austrians were part of the same demonology: Hitler, he wrote on another occasion, 'was the posthumous revenge of the Hapsburgs on the Prussia of Frederick the Great, and on the Germany of Bismarck: he piped them to their doom along paths once blazed out by the Hapsburgs.'[41]

How should we react to Namier's extreme anti-German phobia? And how far does his uncompromising insistence on Germany's culpability in two world wars detract from the value of his historical work, in particular from his *Diplomatic Prelude 1938–1939* (1948), *Europe in Decay: A Study in Disintegration 1936–1940* (1950), and *In the Nazi Era* (1952)? In considering these questions we need to remember that before the mid-1960s many other Western historians expressed broadly similar views. G.L.Mosse, Fritz Fischer and F.L.Stern, for example, also argued that there were continuities between Germany's earlier history and National Socialism, while a plethora of British scholars – Alan Bullock, Hugh Trevor-Roper, John Wheeler-Bennett and Elizabeth Wiskemann among them – stressed the longevity of Germany's expansionist ambitions, and consequently its prime responsibility for the outbreak of war. Only when immediate post-war antagonisms had receded somewhat, and scholars were able to gain fuller access to German and Allied documents, did a more subtle and variegated approach to the Nazi regime begin to emerge. Even today, historians are bitterly divided over whether Nazism was connected to deeper structures and continuities in German history (as Namier contended), or whether the events of 1933 to 1945 should instead be regarded as *sui generis* (as many conservative historians in and outside Germany now claim).[42]

Yet it is also the case that, even when Namier's approach to German history was in the ascendant, some authorities took issue with his excessive zeal. In 1954 D. Cameron Watt published an important article attacking his three books on the Second World War, and accusing him of behaving like a prosecuting counsel, judge and jury rather than as a scholarly historian.[43] Namier was obviously right to condemn the Nazis and their auxiliaries, Watt argued, but objective historians had a duty to analyse and distinguish the motives of the men and women they described, not merely to denounce them as evil. Similarly Namier was clearly correct in retrospect to dismiss Chamberlain's policy of appeasement. But a responsible historian would have tried to explain why that policy appealed to so many Britons for so long. Namier had entirely failed to do this. Instead, he had portrayed inter-war Germany as being intent throughout on European hegemony, and consequently presented Chamberlain and his allies as pusillanimous and stupid for failing to recognize this. He had shown no appreciation of the strategic and economic constraints on British foreign policy in the 1930s, no awareness of the fact that Chamberlain had to confront not only Hitler in Central Europe, but also Mussolini's threat to the Mediterranean and Japan's ambitions in the Far East.

There is no doubt that Watt and those other scholars who have revised our understanding of appeasement are correct in many of their criticisms of Namier. His approach to the Second World War was distorted by evident and multi-faceted bias. To begin with, there was his hatred of Germany, which was connected with both his Jewishness and his Polish origins. Secondly, Namier's historial judgement was coloured by his warm admiration for Chamberlain's great critic, Winston Churchill, and by his own experience in the Foreign Office during the First World War. Both of these circumstances led him to adopt an inflated notion of Britain's room for diplomatic and naval manoeuvre in the 1930s, and to believe (almost certainly erroneously) that this country could still single-handedly intervene to maintain the balance of power in Europe.

Nor was this the full extent of Namier's prejudice. His involvement in the negotiations for a Jewish state in the 1930s had left him with a marked animus against various British politicians and Foreign Office officials, and with the belief that the country's public life was in a state of decay: 'I don't want to see any more ministers ... or anyone of that tribe,' he grumbled to A.J.P.Taylor in 1939. 'Their consciences and their smiles are all made of rubber.'[44] A similar tone of disillusionment and contempt often surfaces in his published work on Britain's pre-war diplomacy:

> The official 'Conservative' leaders of 1938–1939 were mostly ex- or semi-Liberals of middle-class Nonconformist extraction, whose Liberalism had gone rancid – anxious business men lacking imagination and understanding even in business, and in foreign politics lay preachers full of goodwill *à bon marché*.[45]

The snobbery here is evident. As we have seen, one of Namier's complaints against modern nationalism was that it had swept away Europe's traditional ruling aristocracies. He believed quite genuinely that the outbreak of the Second World War could be partly accounted for by the fact that European states were no longer controlled by their *ancien régimes*. He pointed out, for example, that 'the makers and leaders of the Third Reich were Austrians, Bavarians, and Rhinelanders ... not one member of the old [Prussian] ruling class among them.' Conversely, he argued, a high proportion of those Germans who had conspired to overthrow Hitler in July 1944 were of aristocratic or gentry background. (Though why most of these patricians had not seen fit to oppose the Nazi regime earlier than this, Namier never explained.)[46] If the *parvenus* who had risen to power in pre-war Germany were evil, their British counterparts were criminally inept and naive. His comment on Sir Nevile Henderson's conversation with Hitler in August 1939 was typically harsh: 'the reader can hardly help wondering at the level to which the talk of so-called great men can sink since social levelling has wide opened the road to talent.'[47]

This was special pleading and not history. Namier was allowing his judgement to be distorted by his rather pathetic desire to serve as an apologist for elite groups from which he himself was excluded. Thus he made much of those British politicians of patrician background who were anti-appeasement in the 1930s – Churchill, Viscount Cranborne and Anthony Eden. But he failed to mention the many British patricians who were pro-appeasement and in some cases pro-Hitler at this time: Lothian, Halifax, Londonderry, Buccleuch, Bedford and some of the Mitfords.[48] His thesis that Europe slid into a Second World War because it had previously succumbed to a synthetic ruling class was, in short, just one more example of his passionate bias.

Yet despite Namier's preconceptions and limited evidence – perhaps indeed because of these things – his writings on the Second World War and its genesis still retain value and power. This is particularly true of the analyses of foreign affairs he produced in the 1930s. Unlike many other conservatives, he had recognized the significance of Hitler's *Mein Kampf* as soon as it appeared, and from the beginning of this decade he repeatedly warned in print against the rise of Nazism.[49] He was never distracted from this threat – as so many British politicians and patricians were – by fear of Soviet

Russia: indeed, he advocated an Anglo-Russian alliance against Germany. The reason why he felt able to do this was typical of the man. He did not fear Russian ambitions because he simply could not believe that any politician would take Marxist or Bolshevik notions seriously. Germany by contrast was dangerous not primarily because of Fascism, which was merely a doctrine, but because that country was the psychotic of Europe. 'States, like planets, move in predestined courses':[50] Germany could never change its own inherent evil; it was forever trapped within it.

Extreme and emotional though this belief was, it enabled Namier to discuss pre-war European developments far more accurately and presciently – as it turned out – than many more liberal historians. At a time when unreason and intolerance abounded, prejudice like Namier's could be a historiographical asset while cool rationality was left stranded by events.

Namier, then, became a distinctive and indeed a distinguished historian not because he was free of preconceived ideas, but rather because the reverse was the case. He brought a rich variety of concepts and prejudices to bear on subjects which had rarely been approached in this way before. As Peter Gay has written with regard to Gibbon, Ranke, Macaulay and Burkhardt: 'Private perspectives can be, in the right hands, a pathway to historical knowledge ... passion, even prejudice, may provide access to insights closed to cooler, more distant researchers.'[51] So it was with Lewis Namier. The way that he wrote and the content of his writings – his interest in the constituents of social cohesion, in the structure of elite groups and in the psychology of individuals – derived not only from his own academic curiosity and the sources that he examined, but also from the cultural, intellectual and political imperatives of his time. No mind can be independent of the society that surrounds it:

and Namier knew this very well. Even his apparent empiricism – his obsession with hard facts, precise dating and collections of accurate data – stemmed not merely from a commitment to fine scholarship, but also from the positivist tradition in which he had been educated.

His increasing commitment to English history, and particularly to the history of England's political classes, would also be a product of personal needs, of personal imperatives. Namier saw in England a refuge from European complications and a contrast to them. He liked the comparative pragmatism of its politics. He savoured the traditional and settled quality of many of its institutions. Most of all he admired the resilience of its landed elite. 'There is some well-nigh mystic power in the ownership of space,' he wrote in 1930:

> For it is not the command of resources alone which makes the strength of the landowner, but that he has a place in the world which he can call his own, from which he can ward off strangers, and in which he himself is rooted – the superiority of a tree to a log.[52]

It was a superiority of which Namier felt himself acutely deprived. Not only were his people, the Jews, without a territory of their own, but he himself had lost the family estate which had been his personal promised land. How deeply he felt this deprivation may be judged from the fact that in the first flush of his first marriage, he schemed – quite inappropriately given her temperament – to send his wife to Reading Agricultural College. This he hoped would lead 'some day [to] the sight of a well-managed farm in Kent, Herefordshire or on the Lebanon'.[53]

Such bucolic dreams were never realized, and Namier had to content himself with the vicarious sense of security and stability he gained from visiting the great houses of England's territorial magnates and consulting the archives locked away in their stately muniment rooms.

Because his response to these sources was so subjective, because he yearned for land and the assured status that it gave, he was to write about eighteenth- and nineteenth-century England with tremendous originality, commitment and insight. If some of his disciples – the so-called Namierites – were to prove less inspired, it was partly because they only imitated his surface technique. They emulated his empiricism, but not the profound sense of engagement behind it. They forgot that behind Namier's worship of facts, there was always a wealth of feeling.

3 The Political Historian

You must give men new ideas, you must teach
them new words ... you must root out prejudices, subvert convictions, if you wish to be
great.

(Benjamin Disraeli, *Coningsby*)[1]

For Namier iconoclasm was the mark of a great historian. Once he or she had fastened upon a field of study,
'others should not be able to practise within its sphere
in the terms of the preceding era'.[2] It was an appropriate
criterion of greatness for him to adopt, since in both
a general and a particular sense his work substantially
changed the way in which English history was understood. At one level, he attacked the so-called Whig interpretation, which had been the dominant mode of
explaining England's past in the nineteenth century. At
another, he mounted a detailed assault on a particular
component of that interpretation, its virulent indictment
of the reign of George III. To appreciate the magnitude
as well as the limitations of these achievements, we need
to begin by examining the historiographical context in
which Namier worked and against which he reacted.

The Whig interpretation was never as monolithic or as
crude as its critics suggested, but its broad characteristics
are clear enough.[3] As disseminated by E.A.Freeman,
Henry Hallam, W.E.H.Lecky, Thomas Babington
Macaulay and his nephew, George Otto Trevelyan (to
cite only the better-known exponents), it was both
present-minded and intensely nationalistic, concerned to

celebrate Victorian constitutionalism by stressing those episodes of England's past in which freedom seemed to triumph over oppression and injustice. This might involve chronicling the supposed extent of Anglo-Saxon democracy before the Norman Conquest or the barons' efforts to wrest Magna Carta from King John. But many Whig historians preferred to start their story in the early modern period, showing how Parliament had resisted the more extortionate demands of Tudor and Stuart sovereigns, how it had brought Charles I to heel and to the scaffold, and how in 1688 James II's schemes to establish papist and arbitrary rule had splintered in the face of the Glorious Revolution. On this Whig victory was founded religious toleration, Cabinet government, the two-party system and constitutional monarchy: in short, all the blessings that distinguished England from absolutist Europe. But every Eden has its serpent, and England's was King George III. When he came to the throne in 1760, he tried to reassert royal authority as the Stuarts had done. The American colonies were driven into rebellion and into secession from the Empire. In England itself, it was not until the Reform Act of 1832 – naturally a piece of Whig legislation – that liberty and sound government were once again secure.

This version of England's history, transmitted to a massive audience by way of large, confident narratives, was clearly much more than a scholarly fashion. The Whig interpretation was one aspect of English patriotism in the Victorian era, a compound of myths and carefully selected facts which enabled a society undergoing industrial, urban, social, imperial and political transformation to retain its sense of continuity with the past. It is not surprising, then, that some commentators have argued that Namier was able to demolish the Whig interpretation because he was a foreigner. Only a sceptical outsider, it is claimed, could have broken through his adopted country's pieties as ruthlessly as he did.[4] This is a compelling theory but also a misleading one, for the Whig version of the past was under siege even before Namier began to write.

In 1928, just one year before the publication of *The Structure of Politics at the Accession of George III*, H.A.L.Fisher delivered a lecture to the British Academy on the inadequacies of the Whig historians. And in 1931, one year after *England in the Age of the American Revolution* appeared, Herbert Butterfield published *The Whig Interpretation of History*, an elegant if overrated attack on the evils of this method. Thus when Namier embarked on his attempt to retrieve the 'underlying realities'[5] of eighteenth-century politics from the anachronisms and misconceptions that had grown up around them, he was not an isolated and lonely pioneer. Rather he was part of a process of revisionism that can be traced back at least to the 1880s.

It was in that decade that a concerted assault on the Whig interpretation of English history really began.[6] Academic history was becoming more professional, more scrupulous in its attention to archival sources, in short more Germanic. Not coincidentally it was also tending to become more conservative, more ready to approach the rulers of the past in a spirit of acceptance, than to celebrate those who had resisted their authority. Thus in his essays and in *The Expansion of England* (1883), J.R.Seeley criticized other historians for dwelling too much on the achievements of past Parliaments, and for assuming that there was a doctrinal continuity between seventeenth-century Whigs and those of the nineteenth century. Past constitutional conflicts, and 'heroes' such as John Hampden and Algernon Sidney, had been given far more attention than their importance merited: 'history is not concerned with individuals except in their capacity as members of a state'.[7] About the same time, F.W.Maitland embarked on his study of medieval English law, seeking to correct those earlier historians who had looked for legal precedents for the House of Commons; while T.F.Tout – Namier's great predecessor at Manchester University's History Department – argued in lectures and in print that constitutional history was overrated, and that what really mattered was a close analysis of how past administrations had operated in fact and not in theory.

By the time of the First World War, this kind of careful and calculated revisionism was beginning to alter the way in which historians regarded eighteenth-century England. H.W.V.Temperley and W.R.Anson published articles on the Cabinet, arguing that its power and constitutional significance in this period had been exaggerated; and two foreign scholars, the German Albert von Ruville and the American Clarence Walworth Alvord, wrote big and important books challenging the idea that a two-party system had evolved by the Georgian era. 'The attempt to interpret British political history through an assumed rivalry of Whigs and Tories,' Alvord argued in 1917, 'so usual among the older historians, only obscures the truth. Such rivalry did not exist.'[8]

This retreat from heroic, liberal and nationalistic history was a widespread phenomenon at this time. In the United States, for example, the highly patriotic (and consequently fiercely anti-British) interpretation of the American Revolution supplied by George Bancroft in the 1840s and 1850s was coming under increasing attack from the 1880s onwards. Namier would benefit from this American revisionism when he tried to salvage George III's reputation. But although the new, more factual, more unemotional history was by no means a uniquely English development, there were particular reasons why many English historians were drawn to it. By the early twentieth century, the old Whig party was dead; its Liberal successor was in disarray. England, like the rest of Europe, was embroiled in a massive and destructive war. Why, then, should anyone any longer assume that its constitutional arrangements were especially favoured or sacrosanct? Why should England's past continue to be interpreted as a story of fortunate developments and heroic endeavours?

There was certainly small temptation to hold or advance such views in the 1920s when Namier began his sustained study of eighteenth-century England. So although he could certainly claim that the *form* of his history-writing was an experimental and innovative one – a calculated use of structural analysis rather than the grand, narrative manner favoured by the Whig historians – his *approach* to his subject was in line with the widespread disillusionment of his time and with prevailing historiographical fashions. This indeed was partly why his work made such an impact. Great historians tend to be called great not because their writings come as a total revelation, but rather because they address and confirm in some way preoccupations that already exist. This was what Namier did. He wrote non-epic history that was fit for Baldwin's England. What we must consider now is how far his English political history remains fit for today.

Namier was drawn to the eighteenth century because of his consuming interest in the British Empire. From his student days at Oxford, when Lionel Curtis had drawn him into the Round Table movement, he had wanted to explore why the American colonies had been lost.[9] He soon became convinced that the most profitable way of approaching this problem was to study not the colonists themselves but their would-be masters in England. He therefore had no choice but to confront the Whig historians' interpretation of George III's reign – an interpretation which, despite scholarly attacks, was still the conventional wisdom of the time. At its most extreme, it presented George as a turbulent, even tyrannical monarch who deviated from constitutional norms in three crucial respects.[10]

First, he was supposed to have come to the throne in 1760 imbued with archaic and inflated ideas about the extent of royal power. His mother, 'a narrow-minded intriguing woman, with the continental notion of the relations between royalty and the rest of mankind', and her reputed lover, Lord Bute, were supposed to have used their hold over the young prince's affections to educate him in absolutism. He had been nurtured on 'books inculcating the worst maxims of government, and defending the most avowed tyrannies'.[11] Most especially he had been exposed to the writings of Henry St John, Viscount Bolingbroke, a one-time Jacobite conspirator who argued that political parties and contending politicians should be subordinated to the patriarchal rule of a Patriot King.

Secondly, in order to implement these ideas and to restore to the Crown 'that absolute direction and control which Charles the First and James the Second had been forced to relinquish',[12] George engineered the overthrow of the great Whig political families which had been responsible for the Glorious Revolution of 1688 and had dominated English government since 1714. In their place he promoted personal favourites like Bute, and a string of Tory politicians like Lord North. Such men could be expected to share their master's arbitrary ambitions, and together they changed the nature of English governmental practice. At home, activists like John Wilkes were harried and imprisoned for their efforts on behalf of free elections and a free press. Abroad, the thirteen colonies were exposed – in the words of the Declaration of Independence – to a series 'of repeated injuries and usurpations, all having in direct object the establishment of an absolute Tyranny'. George III was thus personally responsible for driving the Americans into revolution.

The King's final abuse of his powers was to employ

corruption on an unprecedented scale. The House of Commons was polluted at source by government interference in general elections. Once elected, large numbers of MPs were bribed to support the King's measures. They formed a group of 'King's friends', a royal party faithful only to George III: 'regarding his personal wishes, carrying out his policy, and dependent on his will'.[13] In this way the legislature, as Edmund Burke complained, was converted into a mere instrument of executive authority. Only a minority of politicians, classically the Rockinghamite Whigs, remained faithful to their party's traditional commitment to liberty and supported the colonists' interests. Had these men been in office, the American Revolution would never have occurred. As it was, their stalwart opposition to the King and to the war with America laid the foundations for a revived and principled Whig party. As George Otto Trevelyan wrote on the eve of Gladstone's great Liberal victory in 1880: 'The nucleus of the Liberal Party, as it has existed ever since, was formed during [this] turbid and discreditable period' – a classic example of how Whig historians could use the past to ratify the present.[14]

This, then, was the Whig case against George III. The King's private virtues might be admitted. Even Sir Thomas Erskine May, whose *Constitutional History of England* (1861) excoriated the monarch, had been prepared to concede them. But his violations of the Constitution could never be forgiven. He had attempted to turn the clock back, to subvert the system of 'responsible ministers, upheld by party connections and by parliamentary interest'[15] which had grown up since the Glorious Revolution, and to make himself as sovereign once more the undisputed head of the executive. As a result, the blame for political chaos at home and for the fall of the First British Empire was emphatically his. 'There is scarcely a field of politics in which the hand of the King may not be traced,' wrote W.E.H.Lecky in the 1880s, 'sometimes in postponing inevitable measures of justice and reform, sometimes in sowing seeds of enduring evil.'[16]

Forty years later, this solemn verdict was still the dominant one among non-specialists. Indeed, when Namier told the Regius Professor of History at Oxford, Sir Charles Firth, that he planned to re-examine the political impact of George III's accession, he was put firmly in his place: Firth 'replied, in his omniscient manner, that Lecky had done all there was to be done about it'.[17] But Namier disagreed. He set out his own alternative interpretation in a succession of books and essays written intermittently from the 1920s through to the end of his life. Inevitably, over such a long span of time, his opinions on some of the issues involved altered perceptibly. Nonetheless, despite its scattered quality and occasional disparities, there is a fundamental coherence in Namier's assault: he reappraised the King; he re-assessed the role of political parties in his reign; and, most impressively perhaps, he reconstructed what corruption was in Georgian England and what it was not.

From the outset, Namier was determined 'to humanize'[18] England's political leaders in the 1760s, to make George III especially something more than the cardboard villain of Whig legend. He scrutinized the King's papers at Windsor Castle, and encouraged a close friend, Romney Sedgwick, to publish an edition of George's early correspondence with Lord Bute.[19] This revealed no settled design to advance the royal prerogative, and no attempt to indoctrinate the young prince in arbitrary notions before his accession. Instead, Namier argued, George's letters demonstrated just how psychologically ill-equipped he was for aggressive political endeavour. He was a lonely and not very intelligent young man, undeniably obsessive, industrious and stubborn, but insecure and if anything too conventional in his views for his own good. Naturally he seemed energetic in comparison with his predecessor, George II, who had been in his late seventies when he died; and, since he was unmarried when he came to the throne, he had initially no male heir to challenge his authority. But in no other significant way, Namier contended, did George III as king differ from previous Hanoverian monarchs. 'What I have never been able to find,' he declared in 1953:

> is the man arrogating power to himself, the ambitious schemer out to dominate, the intriguer dealing in an underhand fashion with his Ministers; in short, any evidence for the stories circulated about him by very clever and eloquent contemporaries.[20]

But if George III's calibre was limited, he remained head of the executive. He had to be, since the Cabinet at this time was a fluctuating and still immature institution, and until the 1820s there were no disciplined parliamentary parties upon which a first minister could rely. Consequently Whig historians were wrong to interpret the rapid turnover of administrations in the King's reign as evidence of his personal impatience of constitutional restraint. No formal, written restraints on the King's right to select his ministers existed at this time. He might in practice be constrained by the availability of talented and experienced men. But otherwise, he could appoint any ministers he wanted and dismiss them as and when he saw fit. Indeed, Namier argued, contemporary politicians such as William Pitt the Elder, the Duke of Newcastle and Lord Hardwicke conceded in their private correspondence that this was the case.[21]

It was true that some opposition spokesmen and politicians, classically Edmund Burke, accused the King of acting in an unprecedented manner. But such complaints did not stem from a profound division of contemporary opinion over the proper extent of royal power and ministerial responsibility. On the contrary, claimed Namier:

Those conflicts of the period which seem to be about the constitution itself, should really be described as the result of inevitable maladjustments in the constitutional machinery; and during the period of transition from purely Royal to purely Parliamentary government, these maladjustments were inevitable.[22]

Disappointed ambition also played its part. Burke's political master, the Marquess of Rockingham, had been dismissed from office in 1766. When he and his supporters attributed their exclusion to a new kind of Court intrigue, they were merely acting as a disgruntled faction. Just as George I and George II had proscribed the Tory Party during their reigns, so George III had the perfect right to exclude a group of Whigs from power if he so chose. In short, it was the Rockinghamites and their more radical allies who were seeking to challenge existing constitutional practices, and not the King and his advisers.

Too much reliance on contemporary propaganda had also misled Whig historians about the significance of party in George III's reign. They had assumed from the persistence of the terms 'Whig' and 'Tory' in the political vocabulary of the period that political conflict hinged on a struggle between two organized parliamentary parties with competing ideologies and policies. They had taken at face value contemporary accusations that the King had engineered a Tory revival without properly examining the personnel of either the House of Commons or successive administrations. Namier, by contrast, deliberately ignored polemic and looked at the behaviour and backgrounds of the individuals in power. He found that the election of 1761 – the first in George's reign – returned only about 110 Tory MPs to Parliament, less than one-fifth of the total number. Whereas the vast majority of these Tories never held office under any monarch, men who called themselves Whigs continued to dominate government in the 1760s. All of George

III's ministers in that decade – including Bute, George Grenville, Charles Townshend and Lord North – were Whigs in the sense that they called themselves by that name, and had been regarded as such before the King's accession. Dissidents in England and the American colonies might find it useful to label these men 'Tories', but this was only a tactical device analogous, say, to the practice of branding politicians one does not approve of as 'Communists' or alternatively as 'Fascists'.[23] Since this was the case, and since the description 'Whig' was employed so promiscuously, it was distinctly unhelpful to try to analyse political conflict at Westminster in this period in party terms.

Instead, Namier argued, mid-eighteenth-century MPs could be regarded as falling into three generic types. First, there were the placemen or King's servants, men who held civilian, military, naval or legal posts, or who were in some way indebted to the administration. These were the 'King's friends' of Whig legend. But far from being a personal creation of George III's, they were a political category that could be found in every eighteenth-century Parliament. Duty and self-interest ensured that they normally supported the government of the day, but they were unable by themselves to supply it with a guaranteed majority. Secondly, there were the Independent Country Gentlemen, landowners who owed their parliamentary seat to their acreage and social status, and who had no need or time for political ambition. These were men, in Burke's words, 'with honest disinterested intentions, plentiful fortunes, assured rank, and quiet homes'.[24] If they acted in concert, they were numerous enough to make or break any government. But they were essentially amateurs in the political game, too independent and too individualistic to exert a continuous impact on events. Finally, there were the professional politicians, a talented minority of careerists who viewed parliamentary affairs not as an obligation but as a sphere for enterprise and advancement. Every eighteenth-century administration needed a nucleus of men from this final category; but if it was to endure, it also required royal approval and sufficient parliamentary support from both the placemen and the Independents.

Namier freely admitted that his reliance on structural analysis left him with little time (and less desire) to examine how far MPs and ministers diverged over policy. He tended, as we know, to ignore parliamentary debates and administrative documents in favour of the letters of individuals. The letters of ministers and MPs in George III's early reign convinced him that politics were still viewed in predominantly personal, localist and insular terms. Because so many MPs were wealthy amateurs and no two-party system existed at Westminster, few individuals bothered to formulate coherent views on major issues such as the organization of the Empire or the nature of the constitution. Instead they concentrated on political intrigue, on advancing themselves and their allies, and on keeping their constituents content. Consequently, Namier argued, Whig historians had been wrong to assume that the Rockinghamite faction would have been able to solve the American problem, and just as wrong in condemning the King and his ministers for failing to do so:

> Neither the imperial nor the constitutional problem could have been solved in the terms in which the overwhelming majority of the politically minded public... considered them at the time; but George III has been blamed ever since, for not having thought of Dominion status and parliamentary government when constitutional theory and the facts of the situation as yet admitted of neither.[25]

Namier's final battery against the Whig interpretation took the form of a reassessment of the extent and meaning of political corruption in eighteenth-century England. For many Whig historians, George III's reputed employment of bribery and patronage was only the most invidious manifestation of a protracted failure in public morality. In the reigns of George I and George II, Macaulay conceded, even Whig ministers had been 'compelled to reduce corruption to a system, and to practise it on a gigantic scale'. Indeed, Hallam argued, the sophisticated took such methods for granted both before and after 1760: 'No one seriously called in question the reality of a systematic distribution of money by the Crown to the representatives of the people; nor did the corrupters themselves ... disguise it in private.'[26] Judgements such as these were often founded on the accusations made by eighteenth-century English parliamentary reformers and American patriots, and they reflected of course the Victorians' comfortable belief that political probity was their own invention. Namier's attitude was quite different. 'The first and greatest task of a historian', he remarked in 1931, 'is to understand the terms in which men of a different age thought and spoke, and the angle from which they viewed life and society.'[27] Consequently, he approached the evidence for corruption not with the primary concern of either condemning or vindicating George III and his ministers, but rather as an anthropologist might do.

He showed, certainly, that the extent to which bribes were used to suborn voters, MPs and peers in the 1760s had been exaggerated. The Crown's direct electoral patronage was limited in comparison with that exercised by private individuals. No Treasury money was deployed in the general election of 1761, for example, but over 110 MPs had their elections influenced by peers of the realm.[28] The significance of money payments to members of either House of Parliament had also been misunderstood. Government supporters had (as in most periods of British history) been able to expect secular advancement in terms of office, favours or contracts; but disbursements of secret service money had been restricted to a tiny minority of impoverished men. Thus only a dozen English peers were in receipt of pensions in 1761 and, Namier contended, these might usefully be regarded as noblemen living 'on the dole or on old-age pensions'. This was perhaps a little too generous. John Cannon has shown that while the Crown may have been primarily motivated by charity in making these payments, it also expected its twelve patrician pensioners to attend the House of Lords with assiduity, and to vote in an appropriate manner.[29]

Far more suggestively, Namier employed a wide range of contemporary sources to construct a vivid and novel picture of political morals and customs outside Parliament. To cite just one example, he demonstrated how difficult it was for even a great electoral magnate like the Duke of Newcastle to control all of his pocket boroughs all of the time.[30] Newcastle was technically the patron of eleven borough seats, and in 1768 he tried to impose on one of these – the town of Lewes in Sussex – a candidate that its 200-odd voters did not like. He failed; and even some of his own tenants voted against him. When he threatened to retaliate by evicting them and by withholding favours from the town, he was advised by his friends to desist. And when he glumly announced that he would settle for an apology, some of the recalcitrant voters still remained obdurate despite his money and extensive local property.

Namier's delight in such episodes has sometimes been interpreted as a rather cynical acceptance of eighteenth-century England's political malpractice. But this is quite wrong. He wanted to show that such bribery and coercion as occurred in this society – however shocking it might seem in retrospect – was of only limited importance in maintaining its political system. And he wanted to go beyond facile condemnation and uncover what corruption signified to its participants. Insofar as there was exploitation in eighteenth-century Lewes, and in many other constituencies which were ostensibly under patron control, it was clearly two-way. Not just the voters, but also Newcastle and his fellow electoral magnates, were captives of the system. As Namier argued:

> Corruption was not a shower-bath from above, constructed by Walpole, the Pelhams, or George III, but a water-spout springing from the rock of freedom to meet the demands of the People. Political bullying starts usually from above, the demands for benefits from below; the two between them made eighteenth-century elections.[31]

The implications of this insight were considerable and have still to be fully digested by historians. If electoral corruption catered to demand from below as well as to the interests of those in power, then it was not surprising that there was no Reform Act until 1832. And if eighteenth-century voters were able to use elections temporarily to invert the social order and to extract concessions, then unreformed England could not be regarded as a deferential society in which the masses invariably submitted to their landed superiors.[32] No one, commented Namier (and he was right), goes to the trouble of bribing or treating social subordinates if he or she can bully them or rely on their spontaneous obedience.

We are now in a position to appreciate the scale of Namier's iconoclasm, his 'seismic demolition'[33] of the Whig historians' view of eighteenth-century English politics. In place of George III, the would-be tyrant, Namier had substituted a stubborn, contorted and fundamentally weak monarch who ruled no differently from his Hanoverian predecessors. Instead of a political world in which the Whigs contended for English liberties and American rights against a resurgent and reactionary Tory Party, Namier portrayed a governing elite that was both fragmented and consensus-bound: too affluent and individualistic for a disciplined party system to be viable, or for profound policy and ideological divisions to emerge. Finally, Namier broke entirely with the Whig historians by refusing to sit in judgement on the political corruption that existed in this society. He made it ostentatiously clear that he was interested only in exploring what functions corruption served, and why it was tolerated. How were these revisions received?

At the level of the educated layman and school textbook, their impact has been slight. Glancing at the massive scholarship and copious footnotes that Namier expended on a few years of English high political history, the average reader today may well be tempted to echo A.J.P.Taylor's mischievous comment: 'did it really matter all that much?'[34] Is it really so important, for example, to know as much about Newcastle's opinions of Bute in 1762 as Namier tells us? Did the eighty voters of mid-eighteenth-century Harwich and Orford really merit the fifty pages that Namier devoted to them? Did he not become so absorbed in the minutiae of his subject that he sometimes forgot the wider pattern of events? Questions such as these are understandable and not without substance: Namier was too often diverted from the main road of historical exposition into some fascinating cul-de-sac of archival research. Nonetheless his analysis has extensive implications for our understanding of history. Not only does it illuminate the internal workings of the most powerful European state and the largest empire of its time, but as Namier himself pointed out: 'history of infinite weight was to be made in the absurd beginnings of this reign'.[35] In ways that are still not entirely clear, the antics of George III and his ministers were an integral part of the making of the American Revolution.

Namier's fellow historians have been swift to acknowledge the importance of his work, and have debated his
conclusions furiously for over fifty years. But unfortu-
nately far more attention has been paid to the details
of his interpretation than to its wider implications. In
particular, his analysis of George III has been almost
continuously challenged both by historians who are sympathetic to the King and by those who are not. Two
of Namier's disciples, John Brooke and Ian Christie, have
adopted his vindication of the King but pushed it even
further. Far from dwindling into an insecure and immature manic-depressive as he does at Namier's hands,
George III emerges from their work as 'a shrewd, cultivated, well-meaning, honest individual', and as a sane
one.[36] The apparent bouts of insanity which disabled
the King throughout his reign and kept him in seclusion
for its last decade are attributed not to ingrained mental
instability but to a progressive blood disease called
porhyria.

More commonly, Namier's interpretation has been criticized for being over-indulgent.[37] He had argued that
the King's inadequacies as a young man disqualified him
for political assertion, yet George ruled until 1810 and
became far more experienced and confident in middle
age. He had proved conclusively that George did not
come to the throne with absolutist designs, but this did
not mean – as Namier sometimes implied – that the King
had no designs at all. Indeed, we now know that George
had very explicit political aims. He wanted to free himself
from some of the powerful Whig dynasties which, he
believed, had bullied and confined his predecessors. He
wanted to end the proscription of the Tory Party, which
had endured since 1714, and rule over a political world
free of organized parties. And he wanted (ironically
given his subsequent reputation) to abolish political
corruption. He came to the throne believing, with his
usual lack of originality, that most politicians were

corrupt and self-seeking. Such beliefs may well have been what Namier called them – 'flapdoodle'. But they undeniably inclined the King to treat ministers throughout his reign in a suspicious, intransigent and tactless manner.

Like many other revisionists, in fact, Namier was sometimes so eager to refute established notions that he pushed his own too far. He tended always to interpret the evidence in George III's favour. He stressed, for example, that in 1775 the King went to war with the Americans in order to uphold Parliament's authority over the Empire and not merely his own: that he was 'fighting the battle of the legislature'. True enough. But seven years later, Lord North had to advise the King that the House of Commons wanted an end to the war and the royal response, as Namier quoted it, was distinctly ungracious: 'whatever you or any man can say on that subject has no avail with me'.[38] In other words, the King was indeed willing to support Parliament when doing so coincided with his own opinions. But – and Namier did not make this point – he was much less ready to endorse the will of Parliament when it conflicted with his own.

Namier was being equally selective in his use of evidence when he claimed that the King's right to appoint and dismiss ministers was endorsed by his contemporaries. In reality, many commentators in the 1760s argued that this right was contingent on the monarch selecting men who possessed evident political experience and parliamentary support: and therefore that George III's promotion of Bute, an unpopular Scottish courtier, was a breach of established political conventions. Namier was correct in observing that many politicians conceded wide powers to the King in their private correspondence. But he refrained from emphasizing that there was often a disparity between what these men wrote and how they acted. Almost every leading politician dismissed from office by the King promptly went into opposition. Even North, who served George III faithfully as first minister from 1770 to 1782, turned sharply against him as soon as he was out of favour. 'The appearance of power,' North would write in his opposition phase, 'is all that a king of this country can have,'[39] a remark that is not quoted by Namier.

Namier sometimes forgot the truth of his own argument that constitutional practices in England at this time were uncertain and in flux. This meant that it was wrong certainly to describe George III's attempts to appoint his own ministers as 'unconstitutional'; but it was equally inappropriate to claim, as Namier tried to do, that the King's powers in this area were always and invariably accepted. And of course in attacking the Whig historians' condemnation of the King, Namier and his disciples were in something of a dilemma. On the one hand, they needed to argue that the King had the right to exercise the powers that he did, that he was indeed head of the executive. On the other, they wanted to exculpate him from the disasters of his reign. Yet as Edmund Morgan and Jack Greene have argued, if the King was head of the executive and chose his own officials, then the ultimate responsibility for England's entry into the American War and for the diplomatic and military failures of that war was emphatically his.[40]

Since it is so difficult to reach a definitive verdict on the rectitude or otherwise of the King's conduct, many historians have wisely stopped trying. In the past two decades, especially, scholars have moved away from awarding points to either the King or his opponents – always a rather sterile exercise – and have become far more interested in exploring what was thought and argued on each side and why. Bernard Bailyn, for example, has shown why so many American colonists came to believe that the mother country was conspiring to oppress them, and John Brewer has examined how

English radicals attacked the Court in the 1760s, and how royal propagandists sought to defend it.[41]

This approach to George III's reign relies heavily on printed sources such as newspapers, ballads, sermons, broadsheets and pamphlets, precisely the kind of evidence that Namier himself deliberately neglected. As he wrote in the preface to *The Structure of Politics at the Accession of George III*, the press response to George III and the American problem had often been trite and simplistic: a closer analysis of public opinion (and Namier put inverted commas around this entity) would not in itself clarify the realities of the political processes involved. Quite evidently, we enter here the realm of Namier's own beliefs, particularly about the impact of ideas on political events. He was not, as we have seen, unmoved by ideas: far from it. But he retained a somewhat purist view about what constituted ideas. If they were crude, or flawed, or expressed by those who had no place at the political centre then, Namier implied, the historian should not give them very much weight. Just as he believed that the urban masses in 1848 merely repeated the empty slogans of agitators, so he was incurious about the protests of Wilkite crowds and American colonists in the 1760s: such people were the victims of 'radicals who plagued and tortured their more sensible and less articulate contemporaries'.[42]

This was a strangely over-rational response from a man who elsewhere in his history made it clear that he appreciated the force of unreason. It was true that the accusations levelled against George III and his ministers by crowds and propagandists on both sides of the Atlantic were often derivative, ill-informed and false: but this did not prevent them from affecting the course of political events.[43] Indeed the genesis of the American War was steeped in misconceptions, in conspiracy theories and in prejudice, and cannot be understood without them. Since the Whig historians had so often been misled by eighteenth-century propaganda, it was understandable that Namier felt compelled to try and establish what really happened. But his approach created a false polarity between ideas and reality, and robbed the reign of George III of its vital public and polemical dimension.

Similar criticisms can be levelled against Namier's treatment of political groups at Westminster. Dismissing the arguments of the Rockinghamite Whigs as self-interested cant was not an adequate explanation of why these men adopted the particular form of cant that they did. Moreover, by ignoring what opposition and ministerial figures said in Parliament on the major questions of the day, Namier as we have seen reduced politicians to pygmy figures interested only in personal and parochial matters. By definition such matters were likely to predominate in the private correspondence that Namier scanned. But, as Edmund Morgan has pointed out, to argue that English politicians were *invariably* unconcerned about wider issues is to admit that the American colonists were right to rebel:

> The Namierites... have cut the Whigs down to size, but they have cut down everyone else on the British political scene likewise ... The whole effect of the Namierist discoveries, as far as the colonies are concerned, must be to show that British statesmen in the 1760s and 1770s, whether in Parliament or in the Privy Council, were too dominated by local interests to be able to run an empire.[44]

Yet of course, with the exception of the American colonies, the British Empire flourished in the eighteenth century and endured until our own: which scarcely suggests that Britain's governing elite was dominated only by parochial concerns. Once again, Namier was misled and misled others by his neglect of the content of political language and political argument.

It is unfair to claim, however, as some of Namier's critics have done, that he rejected altogether the role of party and party ideas in eighteenth-century England. He supplied a very clever analysis of the structure of political alignments in the House of Commons in the 1760s: politics in the nude, to adapt Herbert Butterfield's phrase. But he never suggested that this structure persisted throughout the century, or that at any time this was all that mattered. Indeed, in 1952 he wrote that it was impossible 'to eliminate party from Parliament'. Whig and Tory divisions, he admitted, remained potent in the constituencies, and even at Westminster 'covered enduring types moulded by deeply ingrained differences in temperament and outlook'. Party names persisted, he conceded feebly, 'for names there must be in a political dichotomy ... even if their meaning is uncertain and their use misleading'.[45]

Observations such as these show how troubled and uncertain Namier was about the role of political parties in this period. There were two main reasons for this. First, he was as anachronistically obsessed with the British two-party system as any of the Whig historians whom he attacked: in his view party was only significant when it formed the basis of either the administration or the opposition at Westminster.[46] Hence his comment – a very revealing one – that in 1750 'there were no parties *in our sense of the term*'.[47] Having proved that this was indeed the case, Namier was unwilling to examine what he called the 'intermediary forms' of party that he knew did operate in mid-eighteenth-century England. He was as always troubled about the connection between consciously held political ideas and political conduct, and he did not want to explore the varieties of party organization that existed at this time or the many links between party groups at Westminster and in the localities. All he could do was acknowledge that political debate in this period was saturated with references to

Whig and Tory parties, without satisfactorily explaining why.

The second reason for Namier's unhappiness on this issue was inherent in his own analysis of the structure of politics in Georgian England. Since he believed that the monarch was in fact as well as in theory head of the executive with undisputed powers of ministerial selection, it was unclear to him what roles a loyal opposition could play or even whether a loyal opposition could evolve at all: 'The proper attitude for right-minded Members [of Parliament] was one of considered support to the Government in the due performance of its task.'[48] Only when the heir apparent was at odds with the monarch – as the eldest son of George III was sporadically from the 1780s to 1810 – could dissidents in Parliament acquire unity and purpose. In a political system dominated by the monarch, effective opposition naturally required a royal figurehead. Although Namier himself did not develop this argument, it has become an enduring component of conservative historians' understanding of eighteenth-century England. But whereas he stressed how opposition groups looked to the Hanoverian heirs apparent for nominal leadership, his conservative successors have tended to argue that it was Jacobitism – adherence to the Stuart Pretenders to the throne – that fuelled serious opposition activity in Britain at least before 1760.[49] In both cases, the monarchical component of eighteenth-century English politics is exaggerated, and the activities of constitutional opposition groups at Westminster and outside are neglected.

Namier himself was always sceptical about the political significance of Jacobitism and, as we have seen, betrayed considerable uncertainty about his own views on party. Some of his disciples and imitators were much less diffident, and applied his negation of party alignments in the 1760s to other periods.[50] Thus Robert Walcott, an American scholar, argued that factions and extended family alignments, and not the dichotomy between Whig and Tory, were the crucial components of political conflict between 1688 and 1714.[51] Some of Walcott's supporting evidence was fascinating and remains so, but from the early 1960s his main thesis came under annihilating attack. H.T.Dickinson, Geoffrey Holmes, J.R.Jones, J.H.Plumb and W.A.Speck produced important books demonstrating the force of Whig and Tory rivalry under the later Stuart sovereigns.[52] From the 1970s, a variety of scholars began to reinsert party into the political history of the mid-eighteenth century, and into the post-1770 period. Only Namier's own decade – the 1760s – has remained largely untouched by these partisans.[53]

Undoubtedly this restraint derives in part from a cowardly disinclination to beard the lion in his den, but it also reflects the fact that the years immediately after George III's accession were exceptional. A new king, new issues, the end of the Seven Years' War, the partial dissolution of both the old Tory Party and of many of the great Whig families, all fostered a peculiarly frenzied and fragmented high political scenario. So the question naturally arises: is Namier's analysis of the structure of English politics invalidated by his concentration on one short, atypical period? Or do his findings have a more general value and application?

We can safely regard Namier's political history as both seminal and suggestive, as long as we remember that it was not remotely comprehensive. He exposed a great many of the fallacies and anachronisms that had grown up around George III ever since his reign, but his own treatment of the King was incomplete and not without bias. He uncovered much that was new and important about the eighteenth-century Court and the House of Commons, but he had hardly anything to say about the House of Lords or about central or local administration.

He illuminated what ministerial responsibility and political parties in Georgian England were *not*, but was much less forthcoming about what they were. His exploration of electoral mores in small and pocket boroughs was quite brilliant, but the county constituencies and the large cities – places where we might expect to find evidence of informed public opinion – received very little of his attention. He analysed the types of eighteenth-century Members of Parliament with great sensitivity, but he sometimes gave the erroneous impression that these types and party alignments were somehow mutually exclusive. Of course they were not. Sir John Barnard and Sir Roger Newdigate, who both figure as Independent Country Gentlemen in Namier's analyses, did indeed vaunt their independence from government funding and influence. But at the same time, they regarded themselves and were regarded by others as a fervent Whig and as a committed Tory respectively.[54]

Namier himself never claimed that his work was exhaustive, and was always aware that concentrating on a short span of time had its dangers. But since so little detailed work had been published on eighteenth-century English politics when he began to write, he felt that there was too much to explain to make a long chronological sweep viable. Nonetheless as early as 1928 he was yearning for an opportunity to analyse change over time, and particularly change in the composition and behaviour of England's governing class. As many of his reviewers noticed, Namier was as preoccupied with the House of Commons as any Whig historian. But what fired his interest was not the Commons as a proponent of constitutional liberty, but the Commons as a microcosm, as a cross-section of the political nation. By analysing its changing membership, Namier believed, historians would obtain an unrivalled insight into the course of social, economic and demographic change in England. So concentration on the political elite did not, as some of his critics have contended, lead him into obsessively narrow history. Instead it enabled him to pass from the pursuits of the political historian into the realms of social history.

4 The Social Historian and Parliament

He was always behind those social scenes which, after all, regulate the political performers, knew the springs of the whole machinery, the changes and the shiftings, the fiery cars and golden chariots which men might mount, and the trap-doors down which men might fall.

(Benjamin Disraeli, *Tancred*)[1]

Namier spent the last decade of his life toiling over the three volumes of *The History of Parliament: The House of Commons 1754–1790*. This involved surveying the electoral records of each of the 314 parliamentary constituencies in Britain at that time, and searching out and writing the biographies of the nearly two thousand men who had sat as MPs. Namier employed three full-time assistants and was able to call on other experts in the field. Nonetheless, he himself probably contributed some half a million words to the project, and – like his helpers – had to work without the benefit of a computer to store and collate the material. So the nine hours he put in every day were never enough. By June 1958 he was seventy years old and there were still 650 biographies to go: 'the burden is becoming too much for me,' he admitted.[2] By July 1960 all but seventy of the biographies were complete, and he began to plan a magisterial survey of his investigations in which he would set down his final vision of eighteenth-century Britain. When he died just one month later, not a word had been written.

The Treasury, which had funded most of the project,

and the newspaper press, which had regularly reported on it, wondered irately why Namier had taken so long;[3] many of his fellow historians merely wondered why he had bothered at all. When the volumes were at last published in 1964 some were still wondering. Why had a historian of recognized genius been so determined to devote his last years to a work of reference? Why had Namier exhausted himself scurrying after minor facts and forgotten MPs like some second Casaubon? 'Bricks are important,' pronounced E.H.Carr, 'but a pile of bricks is not a house. And should the master-builder spend his time in a brick field?'[4] Undeniably, Carr had a point. Yet Namier himself viewed this prosopographical analysis of the House of Commons not as a chore distracting him from his proper pursuits, but rather as the consummation of his particular approach to history. The reasons why he felt this are various but characteristic of the man.

As we have seen, Namier was the child of a positivistic age which found it comforting to reduce large and complex phenomena to more manageable facts. In late Victorian Britain, and in many other Western nations at that time, the practice of amassing information about various categories of individuals, group experiences and institutions, and of publishing it in as many volumes as possible, had been epidemic.[5] Between 1870 and 1900, for example, monumental reference works appeared on the country's past archbishops of Canterbury, its judges, its generals, its Roman Catholics, its Huguenot immigrants and its Oxford alumni. The same period saw the foundation of the *Victoria County History* which began to catalogue the flora, fauna, economy, geography and past of every county in England, and of the Historical Manuscripts Commission which pursued and printed details of as many of the nation's archive collections as it could win access to. Most significantly, this was the era in which the *Dictionary of National Biography* was conceived and commissioned, supplying 'full, accurate, and concise biographies of all noteworthy inhabitants of the British Isles... from the earliest period to the present time'.

Thus when prosopography – 'the investigation of the common background characteristics of a group of actors in history by means of a collective study of their lives', as Lawrence Stone describes it – first became established as a fashionable methodology in the 1920s and 1930s,[6] its exponents had access to an unparalleled array of raw, well-documented, ready-printed facts. They also shared the background assumption that doing this kind of work mattered. Indeed, two of Namier's first collaborators on the History of Parliament project, T.F.Tout and A.F.Pollard, had both been major contributors to the *Dictionary of National Biography*.[7]

Namier's own interest in group biography and especially in the changing composition of elites developed early. It had been fostered by his readings of Karl Marx and by Pareto's lectures at Lausanne. And it had been confirmed when he began work on the American Revolution and studied the head-counting methods employed by American historians like Charles Beard and C.W.Alvord. Instinctively he employed similar methods when he came to write his first books on eighteenth-century England, seeking always to answer the big questions by a scrutiny of the behaviour and backgrounds of individuals. In *England in the Age of the American Revolution*, for example, he inquired:

What acquaintance with the American Colonies had the House in which the Stamp Act was passed?... How many of its Members had been to the American Colonies, had connections with them, or had an intimate knowledge of American affairs? Were any of them American-born?[8]

Like many of his fellow prosopographers – Ronald Syme, for example, whose *The Roman Revolution* (1939) used biographical analysis to explain how the Ancient Roman Republic became an empire – Namier was in rebellion against heroic history. He was reacting against the practice of accounting for political change by reference either to the activities of great men or to major developments in constitutional thought.[9] By focusing instead on the impact of elites, connections and family groups, Namier – like Syme – was acting in conformity with his own conservatism, with the widespread political cynicism of his time and with scholarly purism. The small component parts of a major historical process could, he believed, be verified; generalized interpretations could not. But Namier also had a more idiosyncratic motive for adopting this approach. Prosopography, as he practised it, allowed the upbringing and temperament as well as the material interests of individuals to be considered. It took history and sociology and welded them firmly to psychology. As analysed by Namier, the eighteenth-century House of Commons would take in Freud as well as Marx and Pareto as honorary members.

But, as Namier knew full well, to investigate this institution properly over time required more than his own intellectual convictions and commitment: a prolonged collaborative effort would be needed and so would funding on a large scale. The man who first made these things seem attainable was Josiah Wedgwood, a one-time Liberal imperialist turned Labour MP, who knew Namier well through his work as Chairman of the Parliamentary Pro-Palestine Committee. In May 1928 Wedgwood organised a petition signed by 400 MPs urging the Prime Minister, Stanley Baldwin, to support a scholarly history of Parliament from the thirteenth century onwards.[10] True to British form, this led to the formation of a committee which included John Buchan, T.F.Tout, A.F.Pollard and his fellow Tudor historian J.E.Neale, the American expert on Stuart parliaments Wallace Notestein, and Namier himself.

Their report, issued in 1932 – the centenary of the Great Reform Act – is a fascinating period piece. It surveys the wealth of unexplored material available on the House of Commons from 1264 to 1832, but succeeds in being as much an elegy as a work of academic inquiry:

> We were the first people to govern ourselves through responsible representatives. We may be the last. The institution is so peculiarly English, has been so envied by other nations, and has been so widely copied and discarded and fought over, that the world has come to accept parliamentary government as a symbol of freedom.... [But] there is some danger of Parliament losing its dignity and prestige, even in our own country.[11]

In other words, behind Wedgwood's initiative lay anxiety about the present and not just complacency or even curiosity about the past. At home, Britain was blighted by a depressed economy and severe labour unrest; abroad, it was menaced by rising totalitarianism in Eastern and Western Europe and growing turmoil in its Indian Empire. Increasingly, politicians and pundits were responding to these strains by questioning the validity of parliamentary democracy and the two-party system. For Wedgwood, and for many other members of the committee, tracing Parliament's past constitutional achievements at such a time was profoundly consoling, while commemorating its national significance was almost a patriotic duty. As Pollard commented: 'Parliamentary institutions are a gift horse which some are busy looking in the mouth.' If a full-scale history of the House of Commons could be launched, the British people might be revived by seeing how it had responded 'to the needs of an ever-changing national society, and saved that society from the convulsions and revolutions which still disturb realms not yet inured to Parliamentary language'.[12]

At this point, however, Namier himself felt very differently. He was deeply irritated at finding himself, supposedly the great advocate of colourless, clear-eyed, archival reconstruction, becoming yoked to an exercise in unabashed Whiggism. Insofar as the committee's report had addressed his own research priorities, it had done so only briefly and very much as an afterthought. Uncovering the biographies of past MPs, it conceded, would illuminate 'the connection of class with government'. But, in turn, this was not the objective which primarily interested Wedgwood. As the 1930s progressed, his committee fell apart.[13] Two volumes that he produced on Members of Parliament between 1439 and 1509 proved a costly fiasco; and the Slump and subsequently a world war meant that state financial aid for further parliamentary histories was out of the question. Namier became caught up in Zionist activism and contemporary European history; and Wedgwood himself died in 1943. It was not until eight years later, in 1951, that the History of Parliament Trust was established, with Namier very much in charge.

By this stage his own attitudes had changed somewhat. He was now prematurely old, often ill and frequently morose, and far more in sympathy with the valedictory tone of the original committee report. It had lamented not just the decline of parliamentary institutions, but also the departure from the political stage of the old parliamentary class: 'A wider franchise has tended to exclude from public life... many public-spirited people whose unwillingness any longer to take part in government is a loss to the state.' The younger Namier had been able to shrug off such nostalgia as an irrelevance. But in the prevailing 'lower middle-class atmosphere' (his words) of the new welfare state, he no longer felt able to do so.[14] Allowing the romanticism which had always been latent in his response to the English landed classes to come uppermost, he admitted that he envisaged his three volumes of parliamentary history as a 'commemorative work',[15] a testament to social and imperial glories that had now fled. Even if it killed him, he would turn this *magnum opus* into a worthy mausoleum for England's traditional governing elite – and, of course, into a worthy mausoleum for himself.

In part because their genesis had been so protracted and so confused, the three volumes of *The House of Commons 1754–1790* received a mixed reception when they were finally published in 1964. By the standards of the time, they were expensive – twenty-one guineas; and the initial print run of 1,500 copies proved quite adequate for the muted demand. Some reviewers went so far as to complain that the public had been cheated.[16] Self-evidently, the History of Parliament Trust had been expected to produce detailed surveys of the history of Parliament. Yet these initial, long-awaited volumes turned out to be as deceptively entitled as most of Namier's other works. To begin with, they were not so much a history as a collection of raw material on MPs and constituencies. Admittedly the collection was an expert one, and represented a massive gain on what had previously been available. As Namier's co-editor John Brooke recalled:

When Namier began... there was one scholarly work on the eighteenth-century Parliament, *The Unreformed House of Commons* by Edward and Annie G.Porritt... there were biographies of the leading parliamentary figures; badly edited and incomplete editions of their papers (generally with election correspondence omitted); a few scholarly works on parliamentary reform. No attempt had been made at a comprehensive edition of parliamentary debates since the early nineteenth century; for information about back-bench Members there was little except the pioneering works of local antiquarians; and for the constituencies, one had to turn to the propaganda of parliamentary reformers.[17]

But impressive and original though they undoubtedly were, Namier's researches had also been deliberately restricted. He had totally ignored the House of Lords despite the enormous political and electoral powers exercised by the peerage in his period. And, as he freely admitted, he had confined himself to studying the anatomy of the House of Commons, its composition, its recruitment, the voting patterns and connections of its Members. Neither he nor his collaborators had examined how the Commons functioned as an instrument of government, how it made law and policy, or how it made and unmade administrations. Here was a study of a power elite which dissected the elite itself but left out the power almost entirely.

This, indeed, was always one of Namier's limitations as a historian.[18] He was fascinated by the sociology of elites, and by the intrigues and conflict that took place between men in high office. But he was very little interested in how such men used power once they had achieved it. Consequently, his trilogy on the House of Commons between 1754 and 1790 counts heads, votes, rotten boroughs, franchise levels and bribery petitions but, as one reviewer complained: 'What we do not learn is that for all its warts, Parliament in these years was governing – and misgoverning too – the first power in the world'.[19]

If Parliament's role in the running of the state went largely unexplored, so did its impact on the localities. Many of the constituency analyses in these volumes leave the reader with the impression that, once elected, an eighteenth-century MP could virtually forget the men and women he represented. Yet this was seldom the case. Whether they sat for counties, cities, small towns, or tiny and corrupt pocket boroughs, most Members in this period came under grass-roots pressure to introduce private bills and petitions for a variety of local improvements – enclosures, trade concessions, new bridges or prisons or lunatic asylums or markets or roads. This essential but undramatic constituency work can easily be uncovered in the *Commons Journals*, but Namier and his assistants at the History of Parliament Trust rarely bothered to look. As a result, they often conveyed an entirely misleading impression of the relationship that existed between MPs and voters.

Its treatment of the constituencies was in fact one of the weakest parts of Namier's last great work. Initially, he had wanted to omit them altogether and had only been dissuaded by the Cambridge historian George Kitson-Clark.[20] As it was, he and most (not all) of his collaborators confined themselves to brief descriptions of electoral patrons and electoral management; the sentiments and behaviour of voters, though copiously reported in contemporary newspapers, electoral correspondence, ballads, broadsides and pamphlets, went largely unexplored. This neglect was partly due to pressure of time and space, but it also reflected Namier's conviction that there was no real connection between constituency politics in this period and the political process at Westminster. Until voters became more educated and more nationally aware, he argued, their horizons were bound to be confined to local events and priorities. As proof of this he cited the fact (which was not entirely correct) that in the general election of 1774, the growing crisis in Anglo-American relations was a controversial issue in only ten constituencies.[21] Elsewhere the parish pump predominated, or in the case of Newcastle-upon-Tyne – a large trading city with well over 2,000 voters – the Town Moor.

This was an example which Namier relished and referred to again and again.[22] In 1774 a majority of New-castle's voters were anxious about whether they would retain their traditional right to graze cows on the moor, or whether the city's corporation would succeed in having part of it enclosed. What better proof could there be, asserted Namier, of the dominance of local over national issues at this time? But he was wrong. As a mass of printed propaganda issued in Newcastle on this occasion demonstrates, local radicals seized upon this affair and drew explicit parallels between the corpor-ation's designs on the moor and the central adminis-tration's reputed designs against John Wilkes and liberty at home, and against the American colonists abroad. In other words, this episode showed how urban radicals were beginning to 'educate' the public, persuading them that there was a connection between local oppressions and a supposedly oppressive central government and that both evils could only be redressed by a direct application to Parliament.[23]

Because Namier never investigated the nexus between Westminster politics and provincial sentiment, he found it difficult in these volumes to account for the electorate's growing alienation from Lord North's administration. He was far too good a historian to be unaware of this alienation: indeed he tabulated it precisely. He showed that in the general election of 1780, the metropolis, the English counties and the large boroughs – all the consti-tuencies in which opinion and not just management was a powerful factor – returned 111 Opposition MPs as against only 35 supporters of North's policy of war with the Americans.[24] But he never explained the background to this election result. 'There does not seem to have been any popular opposition to North's policy,' states the brief description of the constituency of Norwich, for exam-ple.[25] Yet that city had already shown its bias by submitting a pro-peace petition to Parliament signed by 5,000 inhabitants in 1778.[26] Namier never discovered this fact, because he and many of his co-workers persistently neglected the kind of sources that would have revealed it.

What was never neglected however was detailed research which could cast light on the individual MPs of the period, however obscure or inarticulate they had been. Namier himself deliberately chose to concentrate on biographies of MPs who were second- or even third-rate, or who were eccentric, or rogues, or in some cases insane. It was John Albert Bentinck (reputed 'to have made some notable improvements in ships' pumps'), Bamber Gascoigne ('he was disliked, and was fully conscious of it') and Edward Eliot ('it was his nature to hesitate and worry and tie himself into knots') he wrote about, and not Edmund Burke. He was prepared to deal with Henry Fox, a corrupt and ultimately insignificant pillar of successive administrations, but not his vivid and vitally important son, Charles James Fox. As for the Patriot Minister, William Pitt the Elder, and his second son who became Britain's youngest ever Prime Minister, Namier ignored them both while compiling a meticulous biography of their mediocre relation Thomas Pitt.[27]

This studious avoidance of great men stemmed partly from self-indulgent perversity and possibly too from an awareness of fading powers. But it was also considered policy on Namier's part. 'The fact that a man was a "very insignificant MP" does not mean that his biography should be kept short,' he had written in 1952:

> Our aim is to give a picture of the House based on these biographies of Members. Their status and character outside is therefore of very considerable importance, and has to be given full weight. The resulting picture will be of a sociological character.[28]

As a statement of purpose, this is revealing. The History

of Parliament Trust had been established to promote study of a political institution. But, in Namier's opinion, social history rather than political history was its essential *raison d'être*. Hence his levelling attitude to the MPs he studied. Whatever their political importance or lack of it, all Members were equal to him because all were part of a sample – and he believed, a representative sample – of the governing elite of the time. Hence, too, his lack of interest in the House of Lords. Membership of that House was hereditary. But membership of the House of Commons, he believed, fluctuated in accordance with social and economic change over time. So by studying its composition over a long period – as the Trust's successive volumes would eventually allow them to do – historians would be able to obtain an unrivalled insight into the course of social mobility and economic development:

> From the analysis of the House through the ages will emerge a social and economic history of the nation such as has never yet been attempted.... The individual biographies when strung together will supply a pattern of the history of families and classes; of their rise and decline.... In terms of country houses and manor houses and vicarages, and counting houses, and finally of workshops and factories can be written the history of this country.[29]

Thus Namier, so often regarded only as a conservative historian intent on the static political process, committed himself in this final project to an almost Marxian analysis of society and to the delineation of change. With what success?

Most historians have either ignored Namier's claims about the sociology of the House of Commons or have dismissed them out of hand. Some of this scorn is justified. In the past a variety of important groups were excluded from membership of the Commons irrespective of their social or economic standing. Roman Catholics, for example, were explicitly barred between 1673 and 1829; Jews and men without a landed qualification were not formally eligible for election until the 1850s; and no woman could become an MP until 1919. Before these dates an analysis of the personnel of the Commons tells one nothing about such groups except that they were disadvantaged. And what of the multitudes of people throughout the centuries who had been too poor, too ill-educated, too apolitical or simply too busy ever to consider standing for Parliament? Such individuals might experience major changes in class relationships and in social mobility, but they were unlikely to register in Namier's head-count of MPs. To this extent, then, his famous claim that 'the social history of England could be written in terms of the membership of the House of Commons'[30] can seem little more than provocative nonsense.

But as a means of uncovering the changing pattern of social arrival and social experience at the top, Namier's methodology remains outstandingly useful. We can best appreciate this if we look (as Namier intended us to do) not just at his three volumes, but at those subsequently issued by the History of Parliament Trust which precede and succeed them chronologically: *The House of Commons 1715–1754* edited by Romney Sedgwick, and *The House of Commons 1790–1820* edited by R. G. Thorne.[31] All of these volumes examine the MPs in their period under certain fixed headings: education, religion, occupation, nationality, marriage and kinship patterns and more. As a result, we are given an unrivalled cross-section of an elite over time. Yet, thus far, surprisingly few scholars have plundered this treasure trove to the degree that its riches merit.

But there are honourable exceptions. What can be

achieved by a skilful exploitation of the History of Parliament Trust's work has been shown by John Brewer, who has recently revised our understanding of the relations between the eighteenth-century English state and the military.[32] Namier himself was interested in this topic, not least because he was always alert to a basic truth that most English-born historians take for granted: 'A great deal of what is peculiar in English history is due to the obvious fact that Great Britain is an island.' It was this accident of geography which allowed English patricians to be less blatantly militaristic than many of their Continental counterparts.[33]

But Namier and his co-workers also demonstrated that the military component of successive Houses of Commons was a substantial one. Between 1715 and 1754 the proportion of MPs who were army and naval officers rose from 12 per cent to 16 per cent. Between 1754 and 1790, one in ten MPs held a commission in the army at some point in their career. In the following thirty years, when the French Revolutionary and Napoleonic Wars were raging, one in five MPs held army commissions; and more than one in two MPs saw some military service in home-based volunteer and militia corps.[34] In other words, and as Brewer has shown, Namier's careful spade-work substantially modifies the familiar notion that the political classes in eighteenth-century England held standing armies in fear and contempt. Rather, the military was tamed and monitored by the absorption of many of its most senior officers into the civilian legislature.

Perhaps the greatest potential use of these volumes, however, is in the light they could cast on one of the most persistent debates in British history: how open to new recruits was this country's elite over time? This problem has attracted many scholars in recent years.[35] Most of them have concluded that the elite remained a closed and narrow one until well into the nineteenth century. Yet strikingly none of them has exploited to the full the copious material produced by the History of Parliament Trust. This is partly because the social and economic historians who naturally dominate this field of inquiry tend to assume that the Trust is concerned with political history only. So instead of borrowing Namier's insight that one of the best and most easily verifiable indicators of social status in the past was a man's election to the House of Commons, they have persistently tried to assess the flux of patrician power by reference to the size and value of landed estates and great houses, a time-consuming and risky undertaking.

If however we do accept Namier's contention that 'membership of the House was a status symbol, a sign that [a man] had arrived at the top, not a means of getting there,'[36] what can we learn from the changing composition of the House of Commons between 1715 and 1820? Most obviously that change did indeed occur. In *The Structure of Politics at the Accession of George III*, Namier had noted how new men were able to penetrate the parliamentary representation of some English counties:

> Of the 44 Cornish Members in 1761 ... 25 were strangers, the majority of them with no Parliamentary ancestry anywhere.... In Devonshire, in 1761, 14 out of 26 Members had no previous connection with the county, in Wiltshire 18 in 34, in Dorset 12 in 20.[37]

The History of Parliament volumes show that, while the influx of strangers lessened in the early nineteenth century, it still continued. In the general election of 1802, nine out of the twenty successful candidates in Dorset were newcomers to the county. Even in Lincolnshire, a much more settled county, one-third of the MPs elected in 1818 were strangers.

Such statistics reflect not only the geographical

mobility of Britain's elite but also the emergence of new forms of wealth within the nation at large. Only forty-three of the MPs elected between 1715 and 1754 were engaged in industry, and throughout this early period there were on average some fifty-eight MPs who were merchants and bankers. But when we come to look at the Parliaments elected between 1790 and 1820, we find that the average number of MPs engaged in industry, banking and commerce has risen to 111. Out of the 2,143 men who at some time sat as MPs during this space of thirty years, 360 – one-sixth – were engaged in capital enterprises other than drawing rents and investing in government stock.[38] And the elite in this period changed not only in terms of wealth but also in terms of nationality. Namier found that between 1754 and 1790 some sixty Scotsmen represented English and Welsh constituencies. But the volumes covering the succeeding period, 1790 to 1820, show that during those years over 130 Scots represented constituencies south of the Border.[39] An elite which had been predominantly English in the earlier eighteenth century, was gradually becoming authentically British.

These facts suggest that at certain levels, at least, England's elite in the eighteenth and early nineteenth centuries remained an open one, that the old landed order maintained its vigour by a partial coming to terms with the new. Namier himself always held this view. He recognized, of course, that land was the enduring basis of Georgian politics. But landownership went in tandem with commercial enterprise and commercial imperatives : 'money was honoured,' he argued in 1930, 'the mystic, common denominator of all values.'[40] Since this was the case, English landlords did not measure their estates as Continental landowners did – by acreage or by the number of tenants – but rather in terms of money rents. Nor did most of them remain entrenched in their rural fastnesses. Instead, they were 'amphibious', moving themselves, their horizons and their cash promiscuously between town and countryside, London and the provinces.[41]

This symbiosis between land and trade was reflected in the political and electoral system. Over 70 per cent of England's MPs were elected by borough constituencies, the bulk of them by seaports or by large and small tradingcommunities. Conversely, the predominantly rural county constituencies returned only a tiny fraction of the House of Commons. A House so composed naturally devoted much of its time to trading matters, and Namier even went so far as to quote W.E.H.Lecky approvingly on this point:

> The prevailing spirit of the debates was of a kind we should rather have expected in a middle-class Parliament than in a Parliament consisting in a very large measure of the nominees of great families.... The questions which excited most interest were chiefly financial and commercial ones.[42]

This emphasis should be a warning against any simplistic description of Namier as a conservative historian. Few people can have admired the English landed elite more transparently than he did. But his admiration never rested on the belief that this was a homogeneous elite hallowed by time: rather he was fascinated by its capacity when necessary to be flexible and porous. And he was too much the Marxist ever to ignore the impact of economic forces on this or any other class. 'On a careful enquiry,' he wrote as early as 1928, 'it will be found that the coming in of American wheat has wrought a greater change in the composition of the British House of Commons than the first two Reform Acts.'[43] Subsequent research on the social and agricultural impact of cheap American grain flooding into Britain from the end of the nineteenth century has proved Namier right.

The fact that Namier's work straddled political history, economic history and social history has not always brought him applause. The narrower exponents in each specialization have occasionally attacked him, and his cross-disciplinary wanderings have sometimes prevented him from being wholeheartedly championed by any one academic constituency. Indeed the saga of Namier's involvement with the History of Parliament Trust and its work helps in many ways to explain why his reputation in life and in death has so often been ambiguous and variable. On the one hand, his championing of prosopography when it was still a new and highly controversial historical method convinced many of his audacity and intellectual significance. On the other, the fact that Namier had the ambition, the contacts and the ruthlessness to turn his private enthusiasm for the personnel of the House of Commons into one of the greatest state-aided historical projects of twentieth-century Britain aroused enormous envy and suspicion among his fellow scholars. Much of the rancour that gathered around him in the final years of his life was due to the widespread belief that his 'squadron' of parliamentary researchers was over-funded, over-privileged and overbearing in its pretensions and organization.[44]

As it turned out, Namier's grand design was never an unqualified success. Both the trilogy that he supervised and the volumes subsequently issued by the History of Parliament Trust (which now cover the years 1509 to 1603, 1660 to 1690 and 1715 to 1820) are flawed and incomplete in the analysis that they provide.[45] Nonetheless, the sheer scale and vision of this enterprise remain remarkable, as do its scholarly quality and potential. At the end of the day, Namier had achieved not a mausoleum but a monument. It was just his bad luck that achievement – like audacity and ambition – is not always the surest guarantee of the approval of others.

Conclusion

A really intensely detailed and penetrating piece of analysis is known to historians all over the world as a 'namierization'.
> (*John O'London's Weekly*, 20 June 1952)

The expression 'to namierize' is a deserved tribute to Sir Lewis's influence.
> (*The Economist*, 12 October 1957)

What they could understand he no longer cared to say; what he could now say they would not understand.
> (Sir Lewis Namier in 1960, as recorded by his wife)

How great a historian was Lewis Namier? How indeed do we measure greatness in a profession that has always been too diverse and too self-critical to have one generally agreed apostolic succession, or one universally accepted standard of excellence? Think, for example, of those two eminent Victorians Lord Macaulay and F.W.Maitland. They diverged widely in their conception of history, in their manner of writing it and in their chosen audience. Yet it would be unwise as well as ungenerous to deny either man the title of a great historian. In Namier's case, however, reaching a definitive verdict is more difficult. He never completed any of the major historical projects that he embarked upon. He never produced a big homogeneous book, but only single or interconnected essays. It may be true that 'whether for better or worse, he caused history to be written differently from the way in which it would have been written had he never lived and worked'.[1] But it is also the case that this ambiguous accolade was granted slowly and reluctantly. More than almost any other prominent historian, Namier has always had an uneven and volatile reputation.

His first two major works, *The Structure of Politics at the Accession of George III* and *England in the Age of the American Revolution* met with good but not ecstatic reviews. Sir Richard Lodge commended his industry in ploughing through the Newcastle Papers ('the rubbish basket of the eighteenth century', as he rather unkindly described them), and D.A.Winstanley judged that although his work left existing interpretations intact, it had 'a permanent value on account of its very limitations'.[2] This muted response persisted into the 1930s. Namier gained a certain following in Manchester, Oxbridge and the Ivy League universities, but most historians continued to write about Georgian England in pre-Namierite terms.[3] In Continental Europe, particularly in France, his impact on scholars was even more negligible. And on the wider reading public, whether in Britain, North America, Europe or elsewhere, he hardly impinged at all.

For proof of this, we need only glance at the august ignorance of Sir Robert Menzies, a near-contemporary of Namier's who was Prime Minister of Australia for eighteen years and a cultivated Anglophile all his life. His memoirs, published in 1967, contain the following passage:

> George III was different. He was clearly determined to play a large part in politics, and did so, on the whole, with disastrous results. He became no more popular at home than he was in the American colonies. His mental capacities seem to have been of a

fluctuating order. He opposed and sought to frustrate his greatest statesmen, such as the Elder Pitt. He had, in effect, a 'King's Party', and intervened in the operations of Parliament with singular lack of scruple.

Even today similar statements abound in school and college textbooks, in newspapers and in politicians' speeches.[4] At this level – of the educated layman or woman – Namier's revision of eighteenth-century English history, like the rest of his work, might just as well not have happened.

This is regrettable. When he made the effort to address himself to the public (and he did so far more often than his purist indictments of popular history and the media might suggest) Namier wrote with imagination and rare polemical vigour. From the 1910s to the early 1940s he produced a stream of reviews and articles on current events for the *Nation*, *New Europe*, the *New Statesman*, the *Observer* and the *Manchester Guardian*. Some of these pieces were included in his collected essays, but most remain locked away in yellowing newsprint and are badly in need of rediscovery. This was journalism of course, but journalism illumined and transfigured by an original intellect and a great gift for the vibrant phrase. Its quality and power demonstrate that Namier was fully capable of communicating his historical insights widely and accessibly; but he never applied this capacity to a full-length book or a general survey.

His journalism came to an abrupt halt after the Second World War when his formal career and reputation as an academic historian reached their zenith. His publisher and consistent champion, Harold Macmillan, became a Cabinet Minister in 1951, and subsequently Prime Minister and Chancellor of Oxford University. His loyal and influential patronage helped to prise open some of the doors which had been closed to Namier for so long. Even Maurice Bowra (who hated Namier) felt obliged to capitulate, and proposed that he should deliver the prestigious Romanes Lecture at Oxford.[5] But patronage was only one factor in Namier's belated professional apotheosis. By now, his distinctive approach to British history had been absorbed by his peers and was being imitated by research students on both sides of the Atlantic. His work on nineteenth-century Europe commanded enormous respect, and his thesis that Germany must bear prime responsibility for two world wars was accepted and adopted by a majority of diplomatic historians.

More widely, Namier was no longer held in suspicion as a passionate advocate of controversial issues, be it Ukrainian independence, Zionism or a historiographical revolution. Instead his name and the kind of history that he wrote had come to be linked with pragmatism, with compromise and with an almost doctrinaire aversion to doctrine. And Namier, now fully the elder academic statesman, encouraged this view. As he wrote in 1953:

Some political philosophers complain of a 'tired lull' and the absence at present of argument on general politics in this country: practical solutions are sought for concrete problems, while programmes and ideals are forgotten by both parties. But to me this attitude seems to betoken a greater national maturity, and I can only wish that it may long continue undisturbed by the workings of political philosophy.[6]

In the bitterly polarized 1930s such sentiments would have been out of place and Namier himself would never have endorsed them. But in Macmillan's Britain, as in Eisenhower's America, they struck not so much a chord as a symphony. Ideology was now a dirty and dated word, redolent of the Nazi enemy who had just been defeated and of the Communist enemy who was assumed to be still at the gates. The overwhelming Anglo-

American preoccupations in 'the fat fifties' were a realistic peace, comfortable prosperity and a workable national consensus.[7] In this consciously unillusioned climate of opinion, Namier's historical work acquired a vogue and an influence that it had never enjoyed before. The end of ideology – to use Daniel Bell's epithet on the 1950s – seemed to herald the dawn of Namier's pre-eminence. But it was not to be.

The fact that he was now so firmly identified as a historian who denied the potency of abstract political and intellectual ideas extorted its own substantial price. After 1960, the year of Namier's death, anti-idealism and resolute empiricism became much less fashionable. In the next two decades, the former cult figure was transmuted into a bogeyman, an example for many though by no means all scholars of how history should *not* be written. As early as 1964, J.H.Plumb likened Namier to 'some gigantic, myopic caterpillar' unable to see further than the next leaf on the tree, and certainly incapable of envisaging the wood in all its size and significance.[8] But predictably it was the historians of political thought who emerged as some of his sternest judges. Only recently, Quentin Skinner – whose historical studies began in Namier's shadow – looked back in understandable anger:

At the time of which I am speaking, the leading English historian was widely held to be Sir Lewis Namier ... a sarcastic critic of the belief that any social theories (or flapdoodle, as he preferred to call them) could possibly be relevant to the explanation of political behaviour or the processes of social change.[9]

In treating Namier as a dragon that needed to be slain, the political theorists and philosophers at least took him seriously. Far more damaging to Namier's reputation in the 1960s and 1970s was the dramatic surge in favour of social history, because it was generally assumed that in this field his work had no bearing whatsoever. Why should Namier remain a significant figure or even a figure worth refuting when a growing number of Western scholars were committed, in Fernand Braudel's words, to 'transcending the individual and the particular event'?[10] How could Namier's careful delineation of political intrigue and the taxonomy of patrician elites still be thought essential reading when so many researchers were intent only on rescuing workers, rebels, blacks, women, peasants, criminals and other disadvantaged and marginal folk from the condescension of posterity? Increasingly, in fact, Namier was not read; and neither were his books purchased. In the five years between January 1970 and January 1975 total sales of *The Structure of Politics at the Accession of George III* and *England in the Age of the American Revolution* – never very large – fell by almost 50 per cent.[11] Even Julia Namier's fascinating and much applauded biography went out of print in 1976.

Namier's influence did remain strong among political historians, particularly in Britain where the so-called New History never acquired the currency that it enjoyed in France and the United States. Naturally enough this influence was most apparent in publications on eighteenth-century history, but it also lapped over into adjacent periods. Older works such as Douglas Brunton and D.H.Pennington's *Members of the Long Parliament* (1954), Norman Gash's *Politics in the Age of Peel* (1953), and H.J.Hanham's *Elections and Party Management in the Age of Gladstone* (1959) show this very clearly, but so do more recent monographs. The spate of county studies which appeared in the 1960s and 1970s, all seeking to explore how far the English Civil War modified the composition of gentry elites, demonstrate the continuing attraction of Namierite prosopography and its inbuilt assumptions about social and political power.[12] Still more evident is Namier's impact on the small school of conservative historians that grew up around Maurice Cowling in Cambridge – Michael Bentley, J.C.D.Clark, A.B.Cooke, Andrew Jones and John Vincent among them.

Like Namier, these men pride themselves on archival research that is both massive in quantity and restricted in scope to the papers of individual politicians. Like Namier, they tend to concentrate on the intrigues and interactions of small groups within the British political elite. And, far more single-mindedly than Namier, they argue that such groups constituted the only political world that mattered, a world that was closed:

> It was closed to those outside in terms of direct access and influence; it was closed also in that politicians were bound to see more significance in the definite structure of relationships at Westminster, than in their contacts with the world outside.... Explanations of Westminster should centre not at its being at the top of a coherently organized pyramid of power whose bottom lay with the people, but on its character as a specialized community, like the City or Whitehall.[13]

This description comes from A.B.Cooke and John Vincent's *The Governing Passion* (1974), a minute study of the impact of the Home Rule crisis on British ministerial politics in 1885–6. It descends directly from Namier's insistence that the House of Commons was a club connected only tenuously with the electorate. As he wrote in *The Structure of Politics at the Accession of George III*:

> The result of an electoral system is a House consisting of individuals representative, not so much because they have passed through a peculiar and possibly altogether irrelevant system of 'election', but because they belong to circles which are primarily concerned with the

nation's political business and form therefore the political nation.[14]

But although Namier was one of the main progenitors of the 'high politics' school of British history, its practitioners have not always acknowledged the fact. Just as some nineteenth-century Conservative MPs were reluctant to accept Benjamin Disraeli's contribution to their party, so some High Tory, High Church historians today are averse to admitting their debt to an anti-clerical of Jewish origins who borrowed extensively from both Freud and Marx.[15] Among British and American historians of the New Right, this aversion is even more pronounced, and for good reason. They, like historians of other political persuasions in the doctrinaire 1980s, want to emphasize the role of ideas, the content and operation of political language, and the power of religion. These historiographical priorities appear to leave Namier stranded as an isolated, irrelevant and irreverent empiricist. 'Clever but overrated' seems to be the most common verdict on him at present, a good example of how to damn with faint and condescending praise.

But in judging a historian, or any other creative figure, we need to get beyond reputation – an inherently transient commodity – and reach back to what he or she produced. I have argued throughout this book that Namier's work was important, innovative and diversely interesting. This does not mean of course that all of his writings remain equally valuable, or that his general conclusions are invariably definitive. Professional history has become such a massive and competitive business that the finest scholarship can be overhauled and rendered partially obsolete in less than a decade: much of what Namier wrote is now more than fifty years old. Nor is it realistic to expect that the work produced by a historian in the past should be in keeping with today's scholarly agenda. We may find it amusing that Namier's essay 'The Biography of Ordinary Men' turns out in fact to be a plea for more research into minor MPs, civil servants and merchants. But when this piece was published in 1928 such proposals were both novel and comparatively democratic. Most of Namier's fellow political historians were still confining their attention to monarchs, major statesmen and peers of the realm.[16] By the same token, it might be factually correct to criticize Namier for explaining both the First and the Second World Wars in purely Eurocentric terms, but it would also be anachronistic. This bias was common among European historians of his generation: it is not entirely unknown today.

The most serious accusation which can be levelled against Namier is that he was so intellectually formidable, and so prominent at the end of his career, that approaches to eighteenth-century British history different from his own were stifled. In the schools and colleges, many teachers decided that Namier's work was at once too important to ignore and too difficult and detailed to convey to their pupils. It seemed easier to concentrate on teaching British history in the Tudor, Stuart and Victorian eras. The eighteenth century, Namier's century, tended – and still tends – to be quietly omitted or quickly passed over. At university level, Namier's protégés and disciples often propagated his views in a somewhat mechanical fashion, or responded to any challenge to them with angry incomprehension. Only in the last fifteen years have many historians felt able to examine eighteenth-century British society and the distribution and operation of power within it in ways radically different from Namier's own. They have ceased merely to dispute Namier's answers, and have begun instead to pose new and important questions.

But perhaps it is unfair to blame Namier himself for the undue deference which others so long accorded to his work. Certainly it is time, now that a century has passed since his birth, to reach a more balanced assessment of his achievement. After all that can be said against him has been said, there are I believe four main reasons why we must regard Namier as a significant historian. First, he transformed the way in which history was written in terms of argument, standards of scholarship and methodology. Second, he brought to his craft an unusually powerful and cosmopolitan mind and an arresting style. Third, to a degree that is almost without parallel among the major professional historians of this century, he was a profoundly interesting man. Fourth, his writings merit attention because they communicate and are concerned with the decay of the old European order. Reading Macaulay can help us to understand the lineaments of Victorian confidence; reading Namier is one of the best introductions to this century's insecurity, alienation and angst. Let me elaborate on these points in turn.

Namier's European history is often now dismissed and neglected. Yet his work on the nineteenth century remains vivid and suggestive, and his approach to the Second World War has been profoundly – though indirectly – influential. The medium through which this influence has been exercised is A.J.P.Taylor. Taylor has always resented and resisted the suggestion that he was Namier's pupil: and that is surely correct.[17] But the two men were colleagues at Manchester University's History Department in the 1930s, and remained close allies in the 1940s. Both wrote for the *Manchester Guardian*; both were fiercely pro-Churchill and anti-appeasement; both were interested in the same wide-ranging European topics – the fall of the Habsburg Empire, the German problem, nationalism, revolutions, war and diplomacy; and both respected and were informed about each other's work. As late as 1980 Taylor recalled the 'inestimable' benefit he had derived from listening to Namier's

Waynflete Lectures at Oxford in 1947.[18] But in one very obvious way these two great historians differed. Whereas Namier never converted his richly diverse work on European history into accessible narrative histories, Taylor has become England's most prolific and most popular historian of modern Europe. And, to a quite remarkable degree, Taylor has written the books that Namier planned to write: as well as a great many more.

We can see this connection even in Taylor's most controversial work, *The Origins of the Second World War* (1961). This caused a furore when it first appeared because it seemed to be exculpating Hitler. But Taylor had no such intention. Instead he wanted to argue (as Namier had always done) that far from being a uniquely evil individual, Hitler was 'the creation of German history.... He would have counted for nothing without the support and co-operation of the German people.'[19] Like Namier, Taylor gave very little attention to Fascism as an ideology; like Namier, his treatment of most of the statesmen and diplomats who were active in the 1930s was profoundly cynical. The essence of his interpretation of the Second World War, it has been suggested recently, was 'the continuous line of development in modern European history whereby Germany sought to establish its domination of Europe by controlling the centre and the east':[20] and this, as we have seen, was Namier's position also. To point to these similarities of approach and analysis is not of course remotely to imply that Taylor merely borrowed from Namier. But it is the case that Taylor's work has allowed Namier's ideas and insights in the field of modern European history to remain current and widely influential even though the scattered writings in which they were embedded are now largely forgotten.

In terms of British history we can gain an impression of Namier's prominence just by looking at some of the recent books in the field. They may well seek to refute

or belittle him, but this is nonetheless a tribute to the
longevity of his influence. It is, however, more difficult
to appreciate Namier's positive and uncontroversial
achievements, because they have become so thoroughly
absorbed into our approach to and understanding of
history that we take them for granted. No serious scholar
now believes that George III can simply be regarded as
an unconstitutional monarch or, more widely, that
enduring features of the political landscape – Cabinets,
general elections or parties – operated in the same way
in the late seventeenth and eighteenth centuries as they
did in Victorian England. But before Namier wrote,
many did believe these things. Few historians today
would be quite as casual as Sir John Fortescue was when
he edited George III's letters in the 1930s. But had
Namier not issued his scathing and well-publicized
assault on Fortescue's first volume ('151 documents, i.e.
more than one-fourth of the total, are misdated, insuffi-
ciently dated or misplaced'),[21] the impeccable editions
of historical correspondence that we now possess might
well have taken longer to arrive. All good historians and
graduate students now recognize the importance of
archival research: too much perhaps in some cases. But
this recognition owes a great deal to Namier. Of course
many scholars had plundered the manuscripts before he
did. But he was one of the first professionals consistently
to proclaim their importance, and to persuade an army
of disciples to follow his example.

In the case of prosopographical analysis, especially,
we are almost all Namierites now. Whether we study
an aristocracy or a peasant class, a modern American
small town, a nineteenth-century English factory, a level
of bureaucracy in Ching China or a fourteenth-century
French village called Montaillou, we are likely to be interested in its age structure, its kinship patterns, where its
people come from, how they have been educated and
what each of them owns, earns and believes. We try

in Namier's words to deal with 'aggregates otherwise than in vague generalizations; to treat them as entities in which each person retains his individuality'.[22] Namier did not invent prosopography, but – as with archival research – he brought it to the notice of future generations of historians by the frequency with which he advocated it, and by the facility with which he used it in his own work.

It may be no accident that Namier's fellow pioneer in the field of multiple biography was also an outsider in British academe, the New Zealander Ronald Syme. For there can be little doubt that Namier's own exotic background lent his work a peculiar range, inventiveness and richness of texture. Because of what he was, and where he came from, he was familiar with the writings of Marx, Pareto, Freud and Beard. He could understand French, German, Ukrainian, Polish and Russian. He knew something about American history, and a great deal about the past of both Eastern and Western Europe. Very few professional historians based in Britain have been remotely as cosmopolitan as this; and few have written as authoritatively as he did on both British and European history.

Some of his friends indeed felt that he did not go far enough, that there was a strange disparity between his breadth of culture and his frequent absorption in the minutiae of eighteenth-century English politics. This is what E.H.Carr was implying when he wrote that Namier's works were 'an imperfect tribute to his intellectual status'.[23] And perhaps he was right. But even Namier's most technical history reveals an approach that is far more variegated than mere English empiricism. Here, for example, is a passage from the opening of *England in the Age of the American Revolution*:

Correct perception of a psychological fact underlay Sir Robert Filmer's theory: all authority is to human beings paternal in character.... In the life of every man comes a night when at the ford of the stream he has to strive 'with God and with men'; if he prevails and receives the blessing of the father-spirit, he is henceforth free and at peace.[24]

We may regard effusions such as this as embarrassingly self-indulgent or as entirely redundant. But, if we do, we shall fail to understand how Namier worked. Like many other great historians, he consciously used his personal preoccupations and his diverse beliefs to inform (not, he hoped, to distort) his analysis. In this case, his Freudianism, his mysticism and his own unresolved father-complex were being drawn upon to explain the resonance of Filmer's political thought. It is one more reminder that Namier was never a scientific historian *tout court* and rarely tried to be so.

Since Namier was an alien by upbringing and intellectual tradition, his command of written English – which was not complete until he was over twenty – was remarkable. Opinions about the general quality of his prose vary sharply. Some have compared his style to that of his fellow Pole Joseph Conrad; others have dismissed it as gritty and uneven. My own view is that the style is like the man himself, often difficult but almost invariably compelling. We can see this best perhaps in his essays, which are scattered with imaginative phrases and calculated insights: Metternich was a 'classic in an age of romantics'; the Habsburg Empire was 'not a home for nationalities, but a boarding house'; tradition is 'telescoped memory'.[25] And then there are the mystical passages, which can sometimes teeter over into melodrama but which Namier employed to make the reader pause and think – in this reflection on the Hussites' contribution to Czech nationalism, for example:

The man who walks through the streets of the city before sunrise is called a thief by the awakened sleepers, and the forerunner is called a heretic, and the heretic must be burnt.[26]

This image was a deliberate one. All his life, Namier was drawn to heretics, minorities and oddities. In this respect, as in many others, his historical work was part of the man himself. The critic who saw this most clearly was Herbert Butterfield, who disliked Namier's approach to English history intensely but − for that reason perhaps − worked hard to understand the man: 'I see his originality,' he declared in a radio broadcast in 1961, 'not in things that come from the level judgement of a prosaic historian but in things which arose from passionate depths.'[27] Namier was one of the few modern historians − Marc Bloch was another − whose life was as interesting as, and possibly more interesting than, his work. His complex background, his varied political and sexual involvements, his very diverse range of friendships and intellectual contacts, his obsession with psychoanalysis, and his persistent and never entirely consummated love affair with the British Establishment, all detracted from the time he could give to his writing while contributing immeasurably to the content and the quality of what actually appeared.

Of course, like all of us, he changed over time. There is a considerable gulf between the Namier of the 1920s and 1930s, adrift, iconoclastic, consciously the intellectual explorer, and the more mellow but also more disillusioned grandee of the 1950s, beavering over eighteenth-century MPs in the basement of London's Institute of Historical Research. But, as I have already suggested, in one respect he remained consistent − he was always obsessed with lost or disadvantaged causes and characters. As a child he identified with the family servants against his father, their employer and landlord. In the Foreign Office during the First World War he championed the Ukrainian minority's right to a homeland free from either Polish or Russian hegemony. When he became involved with women, they were almost always waifs like his first wife or refugees like his second. When he began to work on British history, he chose to concentrate on one of its most unfashionable periods and on one of its most controversial monarchs. Despite his constant need to be accepted by the British governing class, he alienated its powerful Arabist contingent by vigorously espousing Zionism. Yet when that cause triumphed and Israel was created, he promptly turned his back on his Jewish heritage and became an Anglican. Such persistently perverse behaviour might attract attention in any individual, but in the case of Namier, who has so often been portrayed as a conservative, as a social snob, as pre-eminently a historian of the elite, it seems particularly to require explanation.

The explanation which I have proposed throughout this book is that Namier was both exile and misfit. Some of his problems were circumstantial – loss of country, separation from his family and the early theft of his Jewishness. But while others have suffered similar deprivations and have nonetheless been able to come to terms with a new culture and a new identity, Namier never did. This shaped his life and moulded his history. If he was drawn to embattled individuals like the Duke of Newcastle, if he was envious of stability, security and tradition, and as a result approached nineteenth-century European nationalism and the English landed elite in a distinctive and polemical fashion, if – throughout his work – he was conscious of the subtleties, the self-deception and the psyches of his fellow men, their pathos and their fragility, he owed these traits in large part to his own persistent unease.

This does not mean that Namier was absorbed only in himself – no historian can be that and still produce work of any quality. Rather he saw his personal dilemma as being symptomatic of a much wider tragedy. The

Expressionist artist Oskar Kokoschka once accounted for the fact that most of his sitters were Jews by suggesting that 'they felt less secure than the rest of the Viennese Establishment and were more sensitive to the tensions and pressures that accompanied the decay of the old order'.[28] Namier witnessed the decay of two great empires, the decline of Europe and the dissolution of its established social order, and for whatever reason his writings carry the imprint of those events. Consequently, if his work should ever lose all of its specific scholarly value – and we are a long way off from that eventuality – Namier will still remain a significant historian. Ideologues, optimists, the complacent and the extrovert, may well be repelled by his analysis. But those who doubt, who question and who think will continue to read Namier – and will continue to be rewarded.

Appendix:
Namier's Papers

Like the man himself, these are elusive. Namier burned what he described as 'a lot' of his old papers in June 1940, probably because he feared a Nazi invasion of Britain at that time. His second wife, Julia, seems to have destroyed yet more of his correspondence and family documents after completing her biography. The papers that have survived are scattered in various public and private archives in Britain, the United States and Israel, and possibly also in Eastern Europe.

There is a large collection of Namier's political papers in the Central Zionist Archives at Jerusalem (A312 series). It includes notebooks, correspondence and published articles connected with Namier's work for the Zionist cause, and information on his early interest in Polish Jews as well as his sterling efforts on behalf of German Jewish refugees in the 1930s. Namier's activities at the Foreign Office between 1915 and 1920 and as an informal liaison officer with the exiled Polish government during the Second World War can be reconstructed from a variety of sources at the Public Record Office in London.

When Namier died in 1960, the bulk of his purely historical papers, including fifty notebooks of transcripts, passed to his close colleague, the late John Brooke. In 1973 Brooke deposited some of these with the Lewis Walpole Library, Farmington, Connecticut, USA. I was able to consult the rest while preparing this book (Brooke Papers) but this collection has since been dispersed. Namier's papers and correspondence in connection with the History of Parliament Trust remained in the Trust's possession as late as 1978. I was informed while writing this book that these documents cannot now be traced.

All that remains is a variety of minor deposits. There are Namier letters in the Wallace Notestein Papers and Charles Nagel Papers held at Yale University Library (MSS 544 and 364). The Butterfield Papers at Cambridge University Library contain notes and press cuttings on Namier by one of his shrewdest critics. Constance Babington Smith, Julia's literary executor, retains a fascinating collection of manuscript and printed materials relating both to Namier and to his second wife (Babington Smith Papers). The late Dame Lucy Sutherland's papers contain one of the richest surviving collections of Namier's scholarly and academic correspondence. In due course these will be made available for consultation at the Bodleian Library in Oxford, but I was fortunate enough to be given advance access to them (Sutherland Papers). I also examined some of the stray Namier letters to be found in the archives of Balliol College and among the papers of various twentieth-century British historians: there will doubtless be others that I did not have time to see or that are not freely available.

More details about Namier's early life and family connections may emerge from the new volumes of the Polish National Biography that are currently in preparation. Almost certainly, however, many documents will have perished when the family estate was sacked and occupied in both world wars.

Notes

INTRODUCTION

1. Copy of Lord Boothby's address, 27 October 1960, Balliol College Archives.
2. *Times Literary Supplement*, 21 May 1971; A.J. Toynbee, 'Lewis Namier, Historian', *Encounter*, XVI (1961), 39; A.J.P.Taylor, *A Personal History* (1983), 199; Isaiah Berlin, 'Lewis Namier: A Personal Interpretation', in Martin Gilbert (ed), *A Century of Conflict 1850–1950: Essays for A.J.P. Taylor* (1967), 215.
3. In his *Vanished Supremacies: Essays on European History 1812–1918* (1962 edn), 8.
4. Review by Hugh Trevor-Roper of Namier's *Personalities and Powers* (1955), place of publication unknown.

CHAPTER 1: THE OUTSIDER LOOKING INWARDS

1. London, 1904 edn, 16.
2. Namier, reviewing C.K.Webster's *The Foreign Policy of Castlereagh 1812–15* for *Week-End Review*, 25 April 1931.
3. Julia Namier, *Lewis Namier: A Biography* (1971). This book is also an apologia and covert autobiography, since Namier spent much of the last sixteen months of his life dictating its content. I have drawn on the information it supplies throughout.

4. Lucy Sutherland to Julia Namier, 8 July 1971, Babington Smith Papers. See also Constance Babington Smith, *Julia de Beausobre: A Russian Christian in the West* (1983).

5. Quoted in Lucy Sutherland, 'Sir Lewis Namier', *Proceedings of the British Academy*, 5 (1962), 373. See Paul Robert Magocsi, *Galicia: A Historical Survey and Bibliographical Guide* (1983), and the section on East Galicia in *Encyclopaedia Judaica* (16 vols, 1971–2), 16, 1325–32.

6. Ruth Gay suggested this point to me.

7. H.W.Carless Davis, *A History of Balliol College* (1963 edn), 243: Namier was referring to A.L. Smith.

8. T.H.Frankel to Julia Namier, 18 September 1971, Babington Smith Papers.

9. Jan Romein, *The Watershed of Two Eras: Europe in 1900*, translated by Arnold J.Pomerans (1978), 95.

10. Carless Davis, *History of Balliol*, 243.

11. Eric Daniel Goldstein, 'Britain Prepares for Peace: British Preparations for the Paris Peace Conference, 1916–19', University of Cambridge PhD dissertation, 1984, 68–96, 194–5.

12. A.J.P.Taylor, *A Personal History* (1983), 167.

13. J.H.Plumb, 'Anguished Historian', *Observer*, 16 May 1971.

14. I owe this information to George Steiner, whose father purchased the other three Monypenny and Buckle volumes. See also J.L.Talmon, 'The Ordeal of Sir Lewis Namier: The Man, the Historian, the Jew', *Commentary* (1963), 241–2.

15. See Isaiah Berlin, 'Benjamin Disraeli, Karl Marx and the Search for Identity', *Against the Current: Essays in the History of Ideas* (1979); and Paul Smith, 'Disraeli's Politics', *Transactions of the Royal Historical Society*, 37 (1987).

16. *The Nation*, 15 November 1930.
17. Bodleian Library, MS Eng. hist. d. 341.
18. Throughout his adult life, acquaintances (and not just unfriendly ones) believed that Namier's fears of mental instability might well be justified: Lionel Curtis to Grigg, *c.* September 1913, Bodleian Library, MS Eng. hist. *c.* 807, fol. 26; John Bromley to Lucy Sutherland, 25 October 1970, Sutherland Papers.
19. As reported by Professor Bromley in the above letter to Lucy Sutherland; Julia Namier, *Lewis Namier*, 258.
20. This is a point upon which opinions still differ. Lucy Sutherland, who was a staunch supporter of Namier but also a staunch supporter of Oxford's reputation, wrote in July 1962 that there was 'little doubt' that Namier's 'intense Zionism and the anti-British feeling that it aroused in him at one time was the chief reason why he did in fact not obtain, at any rate the last, Professorship which he was in for at Oxford', Sutherland Papers.
21. *The Times*, 22 August 1960.
22. A.J.Toynbee, letter to *The Times*, 26 August 1960.
23. Rebecca West's response was 'Absurd. It was like complaining that there was too much claret in the world,' *Sunday Telegraph*, 24 December 1972. R.B.McCallum, *The Oxford Magazine*, 28 April 1972.
24. Elizabeth ? to Julia Namier, 26 October 1971, Babington Smith Papers.
25. From Namier's 1941 essay 'The Jews', reprinted in *Conflicts*, 128.
26. Norman Rose, *Lewis Namier and Zionism* (1980); Julia Namier, 'A Turbulent Zionist,' Babington Smith Papers.
27. Isaiah Berlin to Lucy Sutherland, 18 September

1962, Sutherland Papers. His baptism was also the essential dowry for his marriage to Julia.

28. *The Structure of Politics*, 161–2.

29. Their close academic relationship can be traced in Sutherland's papers.

30. Julia Namier's hand-written comment on a letter to her from Christopher Hill, then Master of Balliol, 20 March 1974, Babington Smith Papers.

31. *England in the Age of the American Revolution*, 13.

CHAPTER 2: THE MIND OF THE HISTORIAN

1. London, 1904 edn, 290.

2. Namier, '1812 and 1941', *Conflicts*, 72; 'Human Nature in Politics', *Personalities and Powers*, 7.

3. Taylor, *A Personal History*, 113.

4. Ranke, of course, was much less objective than he claimed to be. See Leonard Krieger, *Ranke: The Meaning of History* (1977).

5. John Kenyon, *The History Men* (1983), 283.

6. 'Junius Again', *Crossroads of Power*, 158–60.

7. Quoted in John Brooke, 'Namier and Namierism', *History and Theory*, 3 (1964), 343.

8. The best surveys of this period are Romein, *Watershed of Two Eras*, and E.J.Hobsbawm, *The Age of Empire 1875–1914* (1987). See also Berlin, 'Lewis Namier'.

9. Richard Hofstadter, *The Progressive Historians: Turner, Beard, Parrington* (1969), 184.

10. Hobsbawm, *Age of Empire*, 275.

11. *Blue Book*, May 1912.

12. John A.Hawgood to Julia Namier, 8 July 1971, Babington Smith Papers.

13. See Martin J.Wiener, *Between Two Worlds: The Political Thought of Graham Wallas* (1971), 70.

Wallas had left the Fabians in 1904 but maintained many informal contacts with the society.

14. Namier, 'Human Nature in Politics', *Personalities and Powers*, 1–4.
15. *Ibid.*, 4.
16. G.S.Rousseau, 'Namier on Namier', *Studies in Burke and His Time*, 42 (1971), 2023.
17. Box marked 'Transcripts', Brooke Papers. See Stuart Raymond Samuel, 'Marx, Freud and English Intellectuals: A Study in the Dissemination and Reconciliation of Ideas', University of Stanford PhD dissertation, 1971, 157–201.
18. As Peter Gay has reminded me, such a reconciliation was not difficult given Freud's own positivism.
19. Namier, writing in January 1952, quoted in Julia Namier, 'A Turbulent Zionist', 122–3, Babington Smith Papers.
20. Box marked 'Newspaper Cuttings', Brooke Papers.
21. 'King George III: A Study in Personality', *Personalities and Powers*, 39–58.
22. *England in the Age of the American Revolution*, 53–5.
23. Quoted in Brooke, 'Namier and Namierism', 339.
24. Communication by Ian Christie, September 1987.
25. 'The End of Napoleon', *Vanished Supremacies*, 11–19.
26. *House of Commons 1754–1790*, III, 540; *Charles Townshend* (1964).
27. Bodleian Library, MSS Eng. hist. d. 341–2.
28. See, for example, Taras Hunczak, 'Sir Lewis Namier and the Struggle for Eastern Galicia, 1918–20', *Harvard Ukrainian Studies*, 1 (1977).
29. 'Nationality and Liberty', *Vanished Supremacies*, 47.
30. 'Basic Factors in Nineteenth-Century European History', *Vanished Supremacies*, 214–15.
31. Eugene Kamenka and F.B.Smith (eds), *Intellectuals*

and Revolution: Socialism and the Experience of 1848 (1979), 4–12. Since Namier wrote, works on 1848 have proliferated. See Peter N. Stearns, *The Revolutions of 1848* (1974), and Horst Stuke and Wilfried Forstmann (eds), *Die europäischen Revolutionen von 1848* (1979).

32. *Ibid.*, 10.

33. Bodleian Library, MS Eng. hist. d. 341. Namier drew heavily on Veit Valentin, *Geschichte der deutschen Revolution von 1848–49* (2 vols., 1930–31), while amending some of Valentin's calculations about the Frankfurt Parliament's membership.

34. Namier, *1848: The Revolution of the Intellectuals*, 31.

35. Namier, 'Nationality and Liberty', *Vanished Supremacies*, 64; *1848*, 124. Cf. Valentin's far more sympathetic assessment and Frank Eyck, *The Frankfurt Parliament* (1968).

36. See Werner E. Mosse, Arnold Paucker and Reinhard Rurup (eds), *Revolution and Evolution: 1848 in German-Jewish History* (1981), 408–9.

37. *Germany and Eastern Europe* (1915), 17 and 73.

38. *Ibid.*, 15–29; 'The German International', *Conflicts*, 34–5.

39. Bodleian Library, MS Eng. hist. d. 341.

40. *Facing East* (1948), 25; 'The Missing Generation', *Conflicts*, 81.

41. Bodleian Library, MS Eng. hist. d. 341. Namier's hatred of the Habsburg Empire as an aspect of German influence helps to explain why he delighted in its fall, despite the fact that it was a bulwark of the old cosmopolitan and patrician European order that he elsewhere lamented. See Berlin, 'Lewis Namier', 224.

42. See John Hidden and John Farquharson, *Explaining Hitler's Germany: Historians and the Third Reich*

(1983), *passim*. I am grateful to Zara Steiner for her advice on this paragraph.

43. 'Sir Lewis Namier and Contemporary European History', *Cambridge Journal*, 7 (1954), 579–600. Watt developed his critique in 'Appeasement: The Rise of a Revisionist School?', *Political Quarterly*, 36 (1965); and 'The Historiography of Appeasement', in Alan Sked and Chris Cook (eds), *Crisis and Controversy: Essays in Honour of A.J.P.Taylor* (1976). See also Paul Kennedy, 'Appeasement', in Gordon Martel (ed), *The Origins of the Second World War Reconsidered* (1986), 140–62.

44. Namier to A.J.P.Taylor, 15 March 1939 (copy), Babington Smith Papers.

45. *Europe in Decay*, 147–8.

46. *Ibid.*, 234–5.

47. *Diplomatic Prelude*, 308. A.L.Rowse, who dedicated his *All Souls and Appeasement* (1961) to Namier, indicatively advances a similar interpretation. Chamberlain and his supporters, he writes, 'were essentially middle class. ... They did not have the hereditary sense of the security of the state, unlike Churchill, Eden, the Cecils. Nor did they have the toughness of the 18th-century aristocracy' (p. 116).

48. Information from David Cannadine.

49. Rose, *Namier and Zionism*, 60–61.

50. 'Prophet and Pedant', *New Statesman*, 25 June 1955; Brooke, 'Namier and Namierism', 346.

51. Peter Gay, *Freud, Jews and Other Germans: Masters and Victims in Modernist Culture* (1978), ix.

52. *England in the Age of the American Revolution*, 18.

53. Namier to A.L.Smith, 24 June 1918, Balliol College Archives.

CHAPTER 3: THE POLITICAL HISTORIAN

1. London, 1904 edn, 548.
2. Quoted in Lucy Sutherland, 'Lewis Namier and Institutional History', *Annali della Fondazione Italiana per la Storia Amministrativa*, 4 (1967).
3. See J.W.Burrow, *A Liberal Descent: Victorian Historians and the English Past* (1981).
4. Herbert Butterfield suggests this in 'Sir Lewis Namier as Historian', *Listener*, 18 May 1961, 874.
5. *The Structure of Politics*, x.
6. This paragraph is based on P.B.M.Blaas, *Continuity and Anachronism: Parliamentary and Constitutional Development in Whig Historiography and in the Anti-Whig Reaction Between 1890 and 1930* (1978).
7. Quoted in Kenyon, *History Men*, 172.
8. *The Mississippi Valley in British Politics* (2 vols, 1917), I, 20–21.
9. On Namier's connection with the Round Table, see Deborah Lavin, 'Lionel Curtis and the Idea of Commonwealth', in A.F.Madden and D.K. Fieldhouse (eds), *Oxford and the Idea of Commonwealth* (1982).
10. The protracted historiographical debate over George III can best be followed in Herbert Butterfield, *George III and the Historians* (1957), and E.A.Reitan, *George III: Tyrant or Constitutional Monarch?* (1964). See also B.W.Hill, 'Executive Monarchy and the Challenge of Parties, 1689–1832: Two Concepts of Government and Two Historiographical Interpretations', *Historical Journal*, XIII (1970).
11. Sir George Otto Trevelyan and Horace Walpole respectively, quoted in Butterfield, *George III*, 124 and 167.
12. Lord John Russell, quoted in *ibid.*, 104.

13. Sir Thomas Erskine May, quoted in *ibid.*, 154.
14. Blaas, *Continuity and Anachronism*, 123.
15. Erskine May, quoted in Butterfield, *George III*, 153.
16. Quoted in *ibid.*, 164–5.
17. Namier to George Clark, 22 December 1925, Bodleian Library, Sir George Clark Papers.
18. *The Structure of Politics*, ix.
19. *Letters from George III to Lord Bute, 1756–66* (1939).
20. 'King George III: A Study of Personality', *Personalities and Powers*, 57.
21. *England in the Age of the American Revolution*, 47 *et seq.*
22. 'The King and his Ministers', *Crossroads of Power*, 78.
23. This is my analogy, not Namier's.
24. *The Correspondence of Edmund Burke*, ed. T.W. Copeland *et al.* (10 vols., 1958–78), III, 381.
25. *Personalities and Powers*, 40.
26. Butterfield, *George III*, 89; Kenyon, *History Men*, 252.
27. Review of Leonard Woolf's *After the Deluge*, place of publication unknown, Brooke Papers.
28. *The Structure of Politics*, 148: cf. John Cannon, *Aristocratic Century: The Peerage of Eighteenth-Century England* (1984), 109.
29. Cannon, *Aristocratic Century*, 97–9.
30. Namier and Brooke, *House of Commons 1754–1790*, I, 26–7.
31. *The Structure of Politics*, 104.
32. This point was made by many eighteenth-century commentators. William Paley, for example, argued that 'Popular elections procure to the common people courtesy from their superiors. The contemptuous and overbearing insolence, with which the lower orders are wont to be treated by the higher, is greatly mitigated where the people have something

to give': Ian R. Christie, *Stress and Stability in Late-Eighteenth-Century Britain* (1984), 54.

33. Ian R. Christie, *Myth and Reality in Late Eighteenth-Century British Politics* (1970), 9.

34. *Observer*, 17 November 1957.

35. Quoted in Butterfield, *George III*, 213.

36. Ian R. Christie, 'George III and the Historians: Thirty Years On', *History*, 71 (1986), 210; John Brooke, *King George III* (1972).

37. See Richard Pares, *George III and the Politicians* (1953); John Brewer, *Party Ideology and Popular Politics at the Accession of George III* (1976), 112–36; W.R.Fryer, 'King George III: His Political Character and Conduct, 1760–84: A New Whig Interpretation', *Renaissance and Modern Studies*, VI (1962).

38. *Personalities and Powers*, 44–6.

39. Quoted in B.W.Hill, *British Parliamentary Parties 1742–1832* (1985), 29. Dr Hill also shows (on p. 34) how Namier pruned his quotations from the Newcastle Papers in order to buttress the case he wanted to make. Pares, *George III*, 47 *et seq.*

40. Edmund S.Morgan, 'The American Revolution: Revisions in Need of Revising', *William and Mary Quarterly*, 3rd ser., XIV (1957); Jack P.Greene, 'The Flight from Determinism', *South Atlantic Quarterly*, 61 (1962).

41. Brewer, *Party Ideology and Popular Politics*; Bernard Bailyn, *The Ideological Origins of the American Revolution* (1967). My own 'The Apotheosis of George III: Loyalty, Royalty and the British Nation 1760–1820', *Past & Present*, 102 (1984) examines the King's reputation later in his reign.

42. From a review by Namier in the *Observer*, 6 July 1930.

43. For a development of this argument, see Quentin Skinner, 'The Principles and Practice of Opposition:

The Case of Bolingbroke versus Walpole', in Neil McKendrick (ed), *Historical Perspectives* (1974).

44. Morgan, 'The American Revolution', 8.
45. 'Monarchy and the Party System', *Personalities and Powers*, 13–38.
46. Namier's affection for the two-party system is nicely conveyed in a letter he wrote to *The Times*, 20 February 1950, attacking the Liberal Party.
47. *The Structure of Politics*, 213 : my emphasis.
48. *Ibid.*, 212.
49. Ian R.Christie, Eveline Cruickshanks and J.C.D. Clark – who have indicatively all been connected at some time with Namier's power base, the Institute of Historical Research – exemplify this historiographical fashion.
50. But there is no monolithic Namierite tradition on the role of party in the eighteenth century. Compare for example the balanced analyses of John B.Owen, *The Eighteenth Century 1714–1815* (1974), 94–122, 277–94, and Ian R.Christie, 'Party in Politics in the Age of Lord North's Administration', *Parliamentary History*, 6 (1987), with the unreconstructed views of Peter D.G.Thomas, 'Party Politics in Eighteenth-Century Britain: Some Myths and a Touch of Reality', *British Journal for Eighteenth-Century Studies*, 10 (1987).
51. 'English Party Politics', in *Essays in Modern English History in Honour of Wilbur Cortez Abbott* (1941); *English Politics in the Early Eighteenth Century* (1956).
52. H.T.Dickinson, *Bolingbroke* (1970); Geoffrey Holmes, *British Politics in the Age of Anne* (1967); J.R.Jones, *The First Whigs: The Politics of the Exclusion Crisis 1678–83* (1961); J.H.Plumb, *The Growth of Political Stability in England 1675–1725* (1967); W.A.Speck, *Tory and Whig: The Struggle in the Constituencies 1701–15* (1970).

53. E.g. J.C.D.Clark, *The Dynamics of Change: The Crisis of the 1750s and English Party Systems* (1982); Linda Colley, *In Defiance of Oligarchy: The Tory Party 1714–60* (1982); Frank O'Gorman, *The Rise of Party in England: The Rockingham Whigs 1760–82* (1975); John Cannon, *The Fox–North Coalition: Crisis of the Constitution 1782–4* (1969). John Brewer discusses the changing language of party politics in the 1760s in *Party Ideology and Popular Politics* but not the workings of party.

54. A point Namier tacitly conceded in his essay 'Country Gentlemen in Parliament 1750–84', when he quoted a press cutting on Newdigate from 1779–81: 'A rank Tory, with an affectation of honesty and independence', *Personalities and Powers*, 75.

CHAPTER 4: THE SOCIAL HISTORIAN AND PARLIAMENT

1. London, 1904 edn, 123.
2. Namier to Lucy Sutherland, 30 June 1958, Bodleian Library, Sutherland Papers; *House of Commons 1754–1790*, I, ix.
3. See, for instance, an editorial in *The Times*, 30 July 1959.
4. 'English History's Towering Outsider', *Times Literary Supplement*, 21 May 1971.
5. For the material in this paragraph see Lawrence Stone, 'Prosopography', *The Past and the Present* (1981), 45–73, 263.
6. This was in the English-speaking world: German scholars had made use of biographical analysis in the nineteenth century.
7. Blaas, *Continuity and Anachronism*, 331.
8. *England in the Age of the American Revolution*, 229.
9. See Dankwart A. Rustow, 'The Study of Elites', *World Politics*, 3 (1966), 690–717.

10. C.V.Wedgwood, *The Last of the Radicals: Josiah Wedgwood, MP* (1974), 166 *et seq*. Wedgwood and Namier had met when they were both members of the Fabian Society.

11. *Interim Report of the Committee on House of Commons Personnel and Politics 1264–1832* (1932).

12. A review of the *Interim Report*, almost certainly by Pollard, in *Times Literary Supplement*, 13 October 1932.

13. For the differences between Wedgwood and the professional historians on the committee see Namier's and Neale's letters to Notestein, Yale University Library, Notestein Papers.

14. Rose, *Namier and Zionism*, 44n.

15. Julia Namier, *Lewis Namier*, 332.

16. See, for example, C.F.Mullett's hostile comments in *American Historical Review*, LXX (1964), 231; *The Times*, 1 May 1964.

17. Brooke, 'Namier and Namierism', 334.

18. As pointed out by Geoffrey Elton, *Political History: Principles and Practice* (1970), 38.

19. Mullett, *loc. cit.*

20. Information from Sir John Plumb.

21. *House of Commons 1754–1790*, I, 75. Cf. James E.Bradley, *Popular Politics and the American Revolution in England* (1986).

22. E.g. in *Crossroads of Power*, 88; *Personalities and Powers*, 84.

23. Thomas Knox, 'Wilkism and the Newcastle Election of 1774', *Durham University Journal*, 72 (1979–80).

24. *House of Commons 1754–1790*, I, 87.

25. *Ibid.*, I, 342.

26. I owe this information to Dr Kathleen Wilson.

27. *House of Commons 1754–1790*, II, 84, 387, 461–6, 491, III, 286 *et seq*.

28. Namier to Lucy Sutherland, 2 July 1952, Bodleian

Library, Sutherland Papers.
29. Julia Namier, *Lewis Namier*, 290.
30. *England in the Age of the American Revolution*, 3.
31. R.Sedgwick (ed), *The History of Parliament: The House of Commons 1715–1754* (2 vols, 1970); R.G.Thorne, *The History of Parliament: The House of Commons 1790–1820* (5 vols, 1986).
32. *A Polity Transformed: War and the English State, 1688–1783* (forthcoming).
33. *England in the Age of the American Revolution*, 6–7.
34. *House of Commons 1715–54*, I, 155; *House of Commons 1754–1790*, I, 138 et seq.; *The House of Commons 1790–1820*, I, 306–13.
35. E.g. J.V.Beckett, *The Aristocracy in England 1660–1914* (1986); W.D.Rubinstein, 'New Men of Wealth and the Purchase of Land in Nineteenth-Century England', *Past & Present*, 92 (1981); Lawrence Stone and Jeanne C.Fawtier Stone, *An Open Elite? England 1540–1880* (1984).
36. *House of Commons 1754–1790*, I, 138.
37. *The Structure of Politics*, 355–6.
38. *House of Commons 1715–54*, I, 155; *House of Commons 1790–1820*, I, 318.
39. *House of Commons 1754–1790*, I, 166; *House of Commons 1790–1820*, I, 328.
40. *England in the Age of the American Revolution*, 12.
41. *Ibid.*, 14–16.
42. *Ibid.*, 33–4; *The Structure of Politics*, 62 et seq.
43. 'The Biography of Ordinary Men', printed in *Skyscrapers and Other Essays* (1931), 48.
44. This lay, for example, behind an attack on Namier by Steven Watson and other Oxford historians when the former came to talk at Keble College in 1953: Lucy Sutherland to John Bromley, 16 October 1970, Bodleian Library, Sutherland Papers.

45. Apart from the volumes mentioned above, the Trust has issued S.T.Bindoff (ed), *The History of Parliament: The House of Commons 1509–1558* (3 vols, 1982); P.W.Hasler (ed), *The History of Parliament: The House of Commons 1558–1603* (3 vols, 1981); and B.D.Henning (ed), *The History of Parliament: The House of Commons 1660–1690* (3 vols, 1983).

CONCLUSION

1. Isaiah Berlin quoted in the *Listener*, 20 May 1982, 19.
2. Lodge's review of *The Structure of Politics*, in *History*, XIV (1929–30), 269–70; Winstanley's review of the same book in *English Historical Review*, 44 (1929), 657–60.
3. Kenyon, *History Men*, 257–9; G.R.Crosby, 'George III: Historians and a Royal Reputation', in *Essays in Modern English History in Honour of Wilbur Cortez Abbott* (1971 reprint).
4. Sir Robert Menzies, *Afternoon Light* (1967), 250. Cf. John Brooke's comments in *George III*, 17.
5. Undated note by Julia Namier, Bodleian Library, Sutherland Papers.
6. 'Human Nature in Politics', *Personalities and Powers*, 7.
7. See Daniel Bell, *The End of Ideology* (1964), *passim*.
8. *New York Review of Books*, 3 December 1964.
9. Quentin Skinner (ed), *The Return of Grand Theory in the Human Sciences* (1985), 3.
10. Quoted in *ibid.*, 179.
11. According to the accounts sent by Macmillans to Julia Namier, sales of the two books totalled 2,177 copies in 1970, 447 in 1971, 524 in 1972, 893 in 1973 and 1,259 in 1974: Babington Smith Papers.

12. E.g. Alan Everitt, *Suffolk and the Great Rebellion* (1960), and his *The Community of Kent and the Great Rebellion, 1640–60* (1966); John Morrill, *The Revolt of the Provinces* (1980 edn).

13. Quoted in Richard Brent, 'Butterfield's Tories: "High Politics" and the Writing of Modern British History', *Historical Journal*, 30 (1987), 947.

14. *The Structure of Politics*, 134.

15. See J.C.D.Clark, *Revolution and Rebellion: State and Society in England in the 17th and 18th Centuries* (1986), 6–7, 12–15, 22–3.

16. 'The Biography of Ordinary Men', *Skyscrapers*, 44–53. For this point, and many other perceptive comments, see John Cannon, 'Lewis Bernstein Namier', *The Historian at Work* (1980), 136–53.

17. See, for example, his denials in his *Politicians, Socialism and Historians* (1980), 9 *et seq.*

18. *Revolutions and Revolutionaries* (1980), 13.

19. Martel, *Origins of the Second World War*, 125.

20. *Ibid.*, 11.

21. *Additions and Corrections to Sir J.Fortescue's edition of the Correspondence of King George the Third, vol. 1* (1937), 3.

22. Quoted in Lucy Sutherland, 'Sir Lewis Namier', *Proceedings of the British Academy*, XLVIII (1962), 382.

23. 'English History's Towering Outsider', *Times Literary Supplement*, 21 May 1971.

24. *England in the Age of the American Revolution*, 27–8.

25. 'Metternich's Doctrine', *Skyscrapers*, 98; *Germany and Eastern Europe*, 124; Julia Namier, 'A Turbulent Zionist', 41, Babington Smith Papers.

26. *The Czecho-Slovaks: An Oppressed Minority* (1917), 7.

27. 'Sir Lewis Namier as Historian', *Listener*, 18 May 1981, 873.

28. Quoted by Ronald Hayman in 'The Glamour of Great Minds', *Independent*, 6 August 1987. Cf. William A. Jenks, 'The Jews in the Hapsburg Empire, 1879–1918', *Leo Baeck Year Book*, XVI (1971).

Index

INDEX